He Has Risen

The riveting, real-life story of an ordinary man and his supernatural encounters with Jesus Christ

by

Scott Madsen

Amazon.com
12.41

Table of Contents

Preface vii

Chapter 1   In the Beginning 9

Chapter 2   God Calls 17

Chapter 3   Coming to Jesus 39

Chapter 4   God Calls Again 47

Chapter 5   The Holy Spirit a Reality 61

Chapter 6   The Devil and His Demons—For Real 77

Chapter 7   Miracles in Motion 85

Chapter 8   The Word Comes Alive 101

Chapter 9   Down in the Valley with Jesus 115

Chapter 10   God Signs with His Blood 131

Chapter 11   Signs, Wonders, and Miracles.............143

Chapter 12   God Commands—Write a Book 155

Chapter 13   Set Free for Service 167

Chapter 14   It Is Accomplished 183

Chapter 15   Endtimes Messages 187

Chapter 16   War on America 205

Chapter 17   Natural Disasters and the Endtimes 213

Chapter 18   A Call to Holiness 219

Preface

The story you are about to read is true in every aspect. This is the testimony of my experiences with the Lord, and it starts with a visit to heaven while I was in a coma at the age of 21. After recovering from my near-death experience, I began having strange and vivid dreams that appeared to be prophetic messages of future events.

At first these messages were personal, revealing life-changing tragedies that would soon take place in my life. The immediate fulfillment of these prophetic messages confirmed their authenticity. These dreams or visions were prophecies sent by the living God of the Bible.

After I came to that humbling conclusion, the visions began to change and focused on endtime events soon to unfold on our planet. The last four chapters are dedicated to these visions from above.

The bulk of the book presents my Christian testimony. It chronicles the many miracles that led me to Jesus and lays an unshakable foundation for faith in Jesus Christ, the King of kings and Lord of lords. He truly has risen and is active in our lives. This book is filled with accounts of miraculous events that prove the validity of this statement.

After reading this book, you can come to one of only two possible conclusions. The first conclusion: This testimony is false and written by someone who has been deceived by

Satan. The second conclusion: This testimony is trustworthy and true, and we are living in the days that will see Jesus return for His chosen and faithful children.

Please examine each event and compare it to the Scriptures, as God has commanded. Test the spirits to see whether they are from God or not. As you read this book, I pray you will come to the only logical truth: This book contains prophetic messages from the true and living God of the Bible.

May God reveal this truth to you as you ponder the words in this book of dreams!

Scott Madsen

♦ 1 ♦

In the Beginning

The 1960s were radical years. Our country was on an "if it feels good, do it" kick. Radical social changes were in motion, and the family structure was being attacked by a new morality that allowed people to indulge their wildest imaginations. Divorce was no longer a shameful word, because our parents were doing their own thing. All you had to do was take a little pill to be enlightened. Marijuana, LSD, and speed became household words, while "tune in, turn on, and drop out" became the mantra of a generation. While parents in America were out boozing it up, their children were in the back room doing drugs and having sex.

In 1962 prayer was removed from our schools, and Darwin's theory of evolution had replaced what the Bible had to say about how it all got started. This left us without morals, without guidelines, and most importantly, without God. Things seemed great. Everyone was laughing and joking and partying, but as a survivor of this era—I graduated from high school in 1975—I can truly say that those days were marred with sorrow and sadness.

Looking back, I can see how easy it was for me to get caught up in the madness. I was what you might call the typical American kid. I was reared in a family of six (four children and, of course, Mom and Dad). I am the second in line after my older brother, Mike. I also have a sister, Tracie, who is two years younger. Our youngest brother, K.C., came along six years later, making up what our friends and neighbors would call the Madsen residence. We were, for that time, pretty typical as far as families go. My dad was in sales and marketing. My mom stayed home with us. We spent our time in the woods, discovering the beauties of nature and imagining we were explorers in uncharted lands.

As the second in line, I was used to being told that I had to stay home with everyone else while Mike, being the oldest, got to go down to the boat with Dad. And though Mike had that privilege, I was without a doubt my dad's favorite. I was what you would call a chip off the old block. My dad was a talker, and so was I. My dad was a salesman, and so was I. I sold Christmas cards door to door and Ziff soap to the ladies in our neighborhood. I was 10 years old. Little did I know my dad was programming me to be just what he wanted, a carbon copy of himself. As a young child, I had no idea that my close relationship with my dad would later be the source of much sorrow and grief. My life was about to take a turn for the worse, as I followed him down the path that is called the path of sin and death. As I look back, my heart is filled with sadness as I remember how I wanted nothing more than to be a good kid and have the love and respect a young man needs so desperately from his father.

Originally from Utah, Dad moved us out of Provo in 1960 to escape the hold the Mormon Church had on our family. We headed due west and drove as far away from Utah as we could get and still have running water. This landed us in Tacoma, Washington. Having escaped the Mormon Church and its influence, my dad was free to choose his own lifestyle. And choose he did! Like most of the families in our neighborhood, we spent our time on pleasurable endeavors—boating, skiing, sports, and of course, parties. As I look back, the one thing we needed most, a relationship with Jesus Christ, was the one thing we never talked about, thought about, or cared about.

Without moral integrity or guidelines, life can get out of control in a hurry. So it's not too surprising to me that by the time I was in eighth grade I was sitting around the kitchen table with my dad drinking beer and living it up. Shortly after that came marijuana, and then, as you might guess, we had to investigate the heavier and more dangerous drugs.

At the time, this out-of control behavior seemed oddly normal. All my friends in the neighborhood were joining in. We didn't feel bad about it, because, after all, we weren't hurting anyone. We weren't shooting up or anything like that; we were just having a little fun. It all seemed fine, especially when my dad brought home drugs to share with us.

On the outside things seemed fine. We were living it up, laughing, joking, and living for the moment. But on the inside, all was not well. I was dying from the inside out.

God's Word says that a man will reap what he sows. This scripture came alive before my eyes, as our family fell apart from within. My dad started running around with other women and left us emotionally scarred as he sought to satisfy his craving for excitement and pleasure. In my anger, I began skipping school to play video games at the local bowling alley. My grades began to fall as I slipped into a state of chronic depression. I used to be the apple of my father's eye, but that relationship changed as our situation got worse. I finally dropped out of sports. I remember having hateful thoughts towards my dad. He eventually left, leaving my mother devastated and us kids angry and confused.

All these troubles took a huge toll on my self-esteem. Out of control and hurting, I began to search for love and acceptance in painful ways. I became very promiscuous. Looking back I see that I was trying to fill a hole in my heart that only Jesus can fill. With no moral upbringing and the free love movement in vogue, I set out to find love and comfort without the slightest hint of shame or guilt. I felt so inadequate as a man and thought that finding "Ms. Right" would somehow make my life complete. So I gave that all my time and attention.

Life for me became one mistake after another as I went through one relationship after another. Nothing seemed to take away the pain in my heart. The harder I tried to fix my life, the more desperate I became. I longed to find peace and stability, but not knowing that God was the only giver of these things, I always felt empty inside. As a result, my high school days were filled with grief and sadness as I pursued the answers to two questions: Who am I? and What does it all mean?

The Bible says: "God so loved the world, that he gave His only begotten Son, that whosoever believeth in him should not perish, but have everlasting life" (John 3:16). This is a fact I was ignorant of at the time, but looking back on it all, I can see God loving me and helping me—through a beautiful lady I happened to call Mom. Without her at my side, I would not have made it through to today. She was without a doubt the best example of love I could find on this planet.

She helped me by not rejecting me as I piled one mistake on top of another. Although her life was broken in pieces, she went to work and stayed positive, knowing that her children's lives depended on her strength. She did what was right in the sight of God, and God blessed her by bringing her a faithful man, Jack Carbone, to be her husband and the leader of our broken family. His solid leadership was a gigantic blessing to us all. His steadfast love brought us healing and hope, and we all seemed to feel that a new chapter in our lives was beginning. I remember the joy of coming home after school and actually being glad to be home! For the first time in my life, I felt optimistic about my future. For me this was truly a new beginning.

When God created the world, He designed the four seasons for a specific reason—each season different from the rest, each bringing a refreshing newness that makes us feel alive. In similar fashion, life has its seasons. The Bible says in the book of Ecclesiastes, Chapter 3, "For everything there is a season, and a time for every purpose under heaven."

Looking back, I can see that even the coldest winters in life have a purpose. For me, my first big winter had passed, and with a new dad and stepfamily, I entered into a time of healing and hope, which I can best describe as springtime.

I was now a junior in high school, and life seemed to be smoothing out a bit. I now had a real father to look up to. He was solid, steadfast, and full of love. This had a powerful effect on my heart, as I realized that the way I was living was nothing more than foolish.

I began to take an inventory of my ways. I took a good look in the mirror and wasn't pleased with what I saw. I started eliminating the things in my life that weren't stable and honorable. First, I quit smoking marijuana. I wasn't taking any pills at that point, and I made a mental note not to. I made an effort to attend school when I was supposed to. I tried to pattern my life after Jack, because he was the kind of man that I always wanted to be. This was for me a whole new beginning. I had come to a "Y" in the road and, for the first time, I had taken the right road.

For me, being on the right road was only half the battle. I soon realized that although I was going in the right direction, you could say that the car I was driving needed a lot of repair. I was wounded, angry, hurt, and depressed. I was unable to forgive my biological father and often fought with him. I was also abusing alcohol regularly and didn't give it much thought. Drinking was fairly common back then, and everyone I knew drank to some degrees.

Last but not least, I still had a huge void in my heart that I was still trying to fill in promiscuous ways. Even though I was off the true path that leads to righteousness, I felt pretty good about things. Not having any religious training, the things I was doing seemed right at the time. Little did I know that God Himself was about to change my opinion on these things.

As I type these words, I can hardly believe that God revealed Himself in such a powerful way to a man like me. At that time I had nothing to do with the things of God. I was living a life that violated God's precious statutes, while carelessly abusing my mind and body without any regret. That is why this story is as beautiful as it is perplexing. But God's Word clearly states that He loved us first. Jesus said, "I have been found by those who did not seek Me; I have shown Myself to those who did not ask for Me." This scripture is trustworthy and true, and the following testimony is proof that Jesus says what He means and means what He says.

My prayer is that you read the following testimony with an open mind. Everything in this book is true, and God Himself will show you this if you ask Him to. I hope that everyone who reads this book will turn to Jesus. My prayer is they find out for themselves and come to the realization that He really did die on the cross and rose three days later. I pray they believe the gospel and come to the understanding that He is coming back soon. I also pray they turn their lives over to the Lord and begin to look toward that precious day when Jesus returns for those who love His appearing.

In Revelation 3:20, Jesus says, "Behold, I stand at the door and knock: if any man hear My voice and open the door, I will come in to him, and will sup with him, and he with Me."

I also pray that God will use this book to get you to open your heart to Him. The Bible says that everyone who asks receives, and everyone who seeks finds. Remember that it does not matter what you have done in the past. Jesus is ready to forgive you and receive you if you will only let Him in.

May God touch your heart to receive the truths that are written on the following pages.

God Calls

For me, graduating from high school was like turning a cat loose in a hen house. I didn't know which way to turn. Being wounded and not focused, I tried odd jobs to fill my time. I worked on the ocean as a commercial fisherman, I worked for a boat-building company, and I even worked as a janitor at a mall. I would drive the street sweeper at night, sweeping up disposable diapers, mounds of cigarette butts, and loads of empty beer bottles. For a young man full of energy, this was like a prison sentence.

I got my first real job, as a portrait photographer, at the age of 20. This was an exciting job. I got to travel from one town to the next. I liked the variety. I made great money— $500 a week take-home. For that time, this was pretty good for an untrained young man. And for the first time I felt I just might make it. The only negative part of the job was that my clients were all babies. Lots of them! Although I have nothing against babies, I found I had to humble myself daily, as I blew bubbles and talked baby talk to the kids while the moms watched with great expectations of beautiful pictures. My days consisted of Big Bird, dolls, and bubbles. I really didn't mind, because my weekly paycheck kept me motivated, and the travel kept me from getting bored.

Life was looking good. My job kept me going. I traveled through the state of Montana, taking baby pictures and seeing the sights. After that, my company sent me to Oregon. This turned out to be like a paid vacation. It was May, and Oregon has some of the most beautiful scenery you can find on this planet. I felt content. I could actually feel a warm sensation in my heart. Not knowing anything about God, I credited this feeling to my circumstances. As I went about my day, the last thing on my mind was God or heaven or anything that had to do with spiritual matters. But I was about to have an encounter with God that would be the beginning of an intimate relationship that has grown more precious with each new day.

I was wrapping up a two-week shoot in the Medford/Ashland area of Oregon. Taking baby pictures is very demanding, and I was planning on having a nice dinner and getting some much-needed sleep. I remember lying in bed with this overwhelming feeling of peace. I was truly happy for the first time in my life. I fell asleep with a smile in my heart and I was sleeping normally when all of a sudden, I found myself in what seemed to be a dream in living color. The wind was blowing, and it seemed so real that even my sense of smell was affected.

I was in a state of full consciousness as if I was awake, so I can easily recall the details in this dream. The events were not erratic and broken as in most dreams. They flowed in perfect sequence, as though planned in advance like a well-written play or movie. In this dream I found myself standing outside my body. I was watching myself as if I was an actor in a movie, reviewing the day's filming to see the final results.

I looked, and to my amazement I saw myself standing inside a large rock. This rock was big enough to cover me completely and my hands were stretched out, touching the inside walls of the rock.

All of a sudden the earth seemed to open up directly below the rock, and from the center of the earth came a blast of fire that shot up like a huge flamethrower. The fire came from the center of the earth, so it was terribly hot and engulfed the rock. All I could see was fire, fire, and more fire. I watched for what seemed to be thirty seconds as the flames engulfed the rock. I was sure the flames had consumed me, and I stood there thinking that nothing could have survived that inferno. Suddenly my eyes began to see more clearly, and I could see through the flames.

Looking into the fire I was shocked to see the rock acting like a huge shield from the flames, and I could clearly see that the fire had no effect on me at all. After a while the flames burned themselves out, leaving only me inside the rock, untouched, and what looked like the remains of a forest after a fire had consumed it. The area around the rock was charred black; the ground was smoldering.

As I stood wondering what this could mean, I noticed a fearful sight coming from the right side of my field of vision. As I looked, I saw a huge wall of water coming straight at the rock. It looked like a tidal wave with a river backing it up, as if a great dam had burst and let out a deadly wall of water that would destroy anything in its path. This river swept over the rock with the power of a runaway freight train. I was sure the wave had washed me away. But to my surprise, the waters just swept by. There I was, in perfect peace, standing inside the rock, anchored to what seemed to be an immovable foundation.

At this point in the dream, all hell broke loose. There was a huge earthquake that shook the earth horribly. Lightning bolts came from dark clouds and blasted the rock. At the same time, and with great force, a tornado moved overhead and brought with it deadly winds and all kinds of debris. Huge hailstones came from the thick clouds and pounded the rock. The hail was on fire and pounded the rock with deadly force. All these things were happening simultaneously. I have never seen such a display of sheer power. The noise from this onslaught was deafening, the sight utterly awesome.

Then, as if by command from above, it all stopped. The sound, the hail, the wind, and the lightning ceased. All that was left was total silence. I stood there watching as the dust and debris began to settle. I was speechless. What had I just seen? What did this unusual dream mean?

As I stood there wondering and watching, my eyes began to see through the dust as it settled. To my amazement, there was the rock, unmoved by this onslaught, and there I was inside the rock, unharmed, looking no worse for the wear.

At this point the scene changed. In the blink of an eye, and with no thought about it, I was suddenly inside the rock, looking out over the horizon. The earth was flat, and I seemed to be looking eastward to the coast. It must have been night, although I could see perfectly. I noticed a light on the horizon overtaking the dark, as the morning sun rises each day to light our path. This light seemed to move much faster than the sun does, however, and in seconds the sun appeared in the distant view bringing warmth and life with it. When the sun was in full view, its light surrounded me like a warm blanket on a cold dark night. Engulfed by this beautiful peace, I felt my heart grow warm. My mind was at total rest.

That is when I heard the voice of God for the first time. From the surrounding light came a voice so awesome that I immediately knew it was the eternal God speaking to me. This voice was as gentle as a dove, and yet it had an authority you could actually feel. The words He spoke sounded like a command, as if He was ordering what was spoken to come to pass, and I knew immediately that nothing in heaven or earth could stop the fulfillment of what I had just heard. These are the words God spoke to me: "My son, the wind is going to blow for you, but then the sun will shine." Immediately upon hearing these words, I knew exactly what they meant. I knew because each word had supernatural knowledge attached to it. I didn't have to ask what it all meant. I knew exactly what destiny awaited me.

He was telling me that I was going to have a hard life. I was allowed to feel the pressure of future burdens, and I knew nothing was going to change this destiny. I could also see that the suffering I was going to endure was going to change my life, and at the end of the suffering there awaited something special that I could not see yet. Then a flood of emotions overwhelmed me. Fear mixed with joy filled my being, and these feelings shook me out of this dream or whatever it was.

Startled and confused, I sat there on my bed wondering what had just happened to me. I knew it was God. There was no doubt about it. But I had never read the Bible, so I had no reference to draw from to try to understand what had just happened or why. This left me with an eerie feeling that soon passed, as my busy schedule dominated my mind.

I had planned my vacation for the Fourth of July weekend, which was only three weeks away. This kept my mind busy, as I had not seen my family for three months, and I longed to spend some time with them. At this point I was unaware that God was planning to visit me again. This next encounter was going to be profound and change my understanding of life.

For those of you who have never read the Bible, you might think someone with an out-of-control imagination conjured up this strange dream. I know the feeling, because I had similar thoughts until my next few dreams and my later reading of the Bible. I went on with my life and forgot all about that first one until I had two more strange dreams.

Having had three encounters with the Lord, I was convinced God was talking to me. Later, after I received Jesus as my Lord and Savior, I found that these unusual dreams were visual pictures of scriptures found in God's Word. This first dream turned out to be a group of scriptures all in one. It was actually a visual picture of Jesus Christ and His role in our lives.

Here are the scriptures I found in God's Word that explain the first dream He gave me:

- "The Lord is my Rock, and my fortress, and my deliverer; my God, my Rock, in whom I will take refuge; my shield, and the horn of my salvation, my high tower" (Psalm 18:2).
- "When thou passest through the waters, I will be with thee; and through the rivers, they shall not overflow thee: when thou walkest through the fire, thou shalt not be burned, neither shall the flame kindle upon thee" (Isaiah 43:2).
- "Enter into the rock, and hide thee in the dust, from before the terror of Jehovah, and from the glory of His majesty" (Isaiah 2:10).
- "For who is God, save Jehovah? And who is a Rock, save our God?" (2 Samuel 22:32).
- When the apostle Paul was giving his testimony about Jesus speaking to him, he said: "At midday, O king, I saw on the way a light from heaven, above the brightness of the sun, shining round about me and them that journeyed with me. And when we were all fallen to the earth, I heard a voice saying unto me in the Hebrew language, Saul, Saul, why persecutest thou Me? And I said, who art Thou, Lord? And the Lord said, I am Jesus whom thou persecutest" (Acts 26:13-14).
- "I Jesus have sent Mine angel to testify unto you these things for the churches. I am the root and the offspring of David, the bright, the morning star" (Revelation 22:16).

- "And we have the word of prophecy made more sure; whereunto ye do well that ye take heed, as unto a lamp shining in a dark place, until the day dawn, and the day-star arise in your hearts" (2 Peter 1:19).

I found a few scriptures that demonstrate that it truly was a message from God. I didn't know Jesus was the Rock. I was unaware that the Bible says that the floods would not overflow you and the fire would not burn you if you are in Christ Jesus. And I surely didn't know that Jesus is the rising sun, the bright and morning star. I found all these scriptures years later.

After I came to the Lord, I asked many Christians if they knew about a passage that spoke of being "inside the rock." The answer quoted was always the same: "And the rain descended, and the floods came, and the winds blew, and beat upon that house; and if fell not: for it was founded upon the Rock" (Matthew 7:2). This is almost a word-for-word picture of my first dream, but no one knew a scripture that described being "inside the rock." It was years later that God led me to Isaiah 2:10: "Enter into the rock."

Every time I get to thinking about the dreams and visions, I am filled with awe. This God we serve is a supernatural God, full of power and mercy. As you read on, keep in mind that the odds of having one dream you could later see in scripture is beyond calculation. God has given me several of these powerful dreams including one depicting the Second Coming of Christ for His Body the church.

At the time I received this dream I had no idea that it was a true message from God. Having zero biblical knowledge, I forgot the dream and turned my attention to my vacation that was just around the corner. I planned on spending the Fourth of July with my family and friends and my mind seemed to be filled with thoughts of home cooked meals and lazy days. The next couple of weeks whizzed by, and in no time I was saying hello to my folks and settling in for a time of fun and relaxation. I was feeling good; my visit was going well. With the holiday just around the corner, I had already made plans to watch the fireworks with my friend Jeff.

With all the excitement, the last thing on my mind was religion, the Bible, Jesus, or anything that had to do with spiritual matters. I was unaware that I was about to have my second visit from the Lord, so I went about my business and focused on family and friends. This particular encounter with God would change my understanding of life and lead me to the highway of holiness found in Isaiah 35:8.

I was staying with my parents because I traveled so much that it didn't make financial sense to keep an apartment. I had gone to bed early anticipating a normal night's sleep and a great time the next day. This night, though, was going to be anything but normal, because I was going to receive a dream from the Lord that warned me of an event that would occur a week later.

I went to sleep early that night and woke to find myself standing on the street corner with two men. They were wearing long raincoats, like the ones secret agents wear when they want to hide their identity. As I watched, a man strolled by and seemed not to notice us as he passed in front of us.

All of a sudden the two men flipped open their raincoats. To my shock, they both had shotguns under their coats. They drew them, and with both barrels blasting, they terminated this man and began running down the street with me following them. A car screeched to a stop in front of us, and we got in. I guessed it was our getaway car so I jumped in the back seat. All of a sudden the man in the front seat pulled out a handgun. He turned around in his seat and said, "Sorry — orders." He then put five bullets point blank into my heart.

Suddenly, this dream went from black and white to color and also changed to slow motion as the force of the bullets blew my body back. I crashed back and could actually taste blood in my mouth, as well as seeing the blood flooding out of my chest. I landed flat in the back seat.

Then an even more unusual thing happened. I knew I was dying, and yet I felt alive, more alive than words can describe. I felt my heart stop, and I left my body without any effort. Suddenly, I could see skyward, and I shot up into the clouds with rocket-like force.

The scene then changed, and I found myself floating inside a cloud that seemed to be alive. It was moving all around me, and it looked like pure thought, if you can envision that. From this cloud came a voice that could only belong to God. I heard it and instantly knew who was speaking. This is what I heard: "My son, I'm going to send you to New York."

Upon hearing these words, I shot due east, and with lightning speed I arrived over a city that I knew to be New York. I found myself floating above a huge circle of people. They represented every nation, and I was in the center of the circle about ten feet off the ground. My right hand was extended, and my finger was pointing down at the people below. Then I began to speak. I only remember some of the words, but I knew I was acting as an ambassador for God. He was putting His thoughts in me, and I was conveying them to the people.

The words I remember went as follows: "God has sent me here to tell you that you need to start loving one another like God commands in His Word. If you do not change, God's judgment will be swift and sure!" With that I woke up suddenly and sat there in the dark wondering what this dream meant.

Over the last twenty years I have had three similar dreams. A man shoots me, and he always says "Sorry—orders." Each time I've had this dream, it was followed by a life-changing event within seven days. I have learned to trust the messages and know these dreams were warnings of hard times ahead.

Looking back I can say that they were prophetic dreams sent by God.

I went through the next day wondering about all this. That night I had another dream that God would not let me remember. All I knew is that it too was about dying, and that it was no ordinary dream. I remember telling my mom that I felt as if something terrible was going to happen to me. Naturally, she did not receive this very well, and I dropped the subject. The rest of the week passed without incident— which brings us to the Fourth of July.

The Fourth started out as any other holiday, but it ended up being anything but normal. Jeff and I set out for Gravelly Lake to watch the annual fireworks display. As we arrived, we met up with some old friends from school and decided to go to Jeff's apartment instead of staying to watch the fireworks.

As we approached Jeff's place, we noticed a car parked in some bushes with the engine running and the driver sitting there motionless. We got out to help him but found that he would not, or could not, speak. He stared straight ahead and did not move at all. We were in Jeff's convertible and were drinking beer at the time. Jumping out of the car, we put our beer cans on the hood of the car, not thinking about anything other than helping this man out of his dilemma.

As we tried to talk to him, something happened that did not make sense. A policeman pulled up, got out of his car, and asked us what was happening. Not wanting the policeman to take him in, we told him that he was a friend who had too much to drink and we were going to take him over to Jeff's apartment.

The policeman looked the scene over as he stood by our car. He saw the beer cans on the hood of the car. We were drunk, and the driver of the other car was obviously out of it. This did not seem to faze this policeman at all. He casually got back into his car, warned us not to drink and drive, and drove off, leaving us speechless. We felt as if we had just gotten away with murder. Why had he let us go when we were clearly drunk? He must have seen the beer cans on the hood of the car, and here was this other car, half in and half out of some ten-foot-tall bushes. This made no sense to us and left us more than confused.

After that, we loaded the man into our convertible with the idea that we would take him to Jeff's apartment and find out where he lived. I drove him in Jeff's car, and Jeff followed in the stranger's Toyota. Then something unforgettable happened. As we pulled into the parking lot, the man suddenly stood straight up and stepped over the side of the convertible while it was still moving. He didn't fall, and as his feet met the pavement, he kept walking. I remember pleading with him to come back, but he kept walking until he was out of sight, never to be seen again.

That night we had what the world would call a really good time. We played drinking games until midnight and were feeling no pain as we said goodbye to each other. That's when the trouble started. Jeff had the keys to the man's car and talked me into taking it out for a burger. We reasoned that it was OK because he let us drive it earlier, and we weren't stealing it but just taking it for a drive. (I obviously wasn't too smart back in those days.) So off we went in this car.

All of a sudden, I heard a voice inside my head say "Drugs!" Instantly I knew that there were drugs in his car. We opened the glove box and found nothing. We looked in the registration holder attached to the car's visor but came up empty. It wasn't until we gave up searching that my arm dropped down, with my hand falling between the car seat and the center console. When that happened, my hand landed on something that crinkled. Before I knew it, we were looking at this little package with some white powder in it.

We went back to Jeff's place and poured the contents of the package on the table. Jeff tasted it and said it was cocaine. I had never tried that particular drug, so I took his word for it as we decided to give it a try. At that time I had long since given up drugs, but I was drunk and caught up in the moment.

After we sniffed all of the powder up our noses, we sat there waiting for that feel-good effect we heard cocaine gave people. What we didn't realize was that it wasn't cocaine. It was a drug called Angel Dust, one of the most dangerous drugs out there. Needless to say, what we thought was going to happen and what actually happened were two altogether different things.

Twenty minutes went by, and we started to feel really goofy. Our minds were drifting further away from reality by the minute. We decided to drive down to the beach to watch the sun come up. By that time I realized I was in real trouble. I passed out and returned to consciousness twice in the space of about two minutes. Then I lost all touch with reality. For the next few hours I was in a coma. I don't remember much after that except hearing a man's voice telling me I was dying. After that I remember being up in a most beautiful blue sky. I saw a place that I knew was a part of heaven.

Waking up out of the coma was traumatic. I was in the hospital and could not remember what had happened. I was a mess. I couldn't see or hear; everything was garbled and I figured that I had been in a bad car accident.

Recovering from this overdose was a painful process. I slept for nearly a week, waking long enough to eat some-thing and then sleeping for five to eight hours. During that time I was deeply troubled. Why had this happened? I felt betrayed by life itself. I had always tried to love people, so why me? And those dreams about dying—they were so real! Here I was a week later, and it looked as if they weren't just dreams. Who was God anyway? Why had He allowed this to happen, if indeed He knew about it beforehand?

That night I went to bed with big questions on my heart. Why was I alive? Who was I? What did life mean? Why was I here? With these questions on my mind, I drifted off to sleep.

Just after 3 a.m., I started to wake up from a deep sleep to find myself in a totally dark place. But this was a warm, safe place, and I felt totally at peace. I realized I had been talking to someone for quite some time but I couldn't remember who I had been talking to or what we had discussed. I do remember asking, "Where am I, and whom am I talking with"? Having asked this question I heard my voice say, "God, why am I here on earth?" Having said these words it felt as if He was answering my question through the words that came out of my mouth. At that time I didn't know if this was even possible.

Years later, I found out that with God, "all things are possible." I found scriptures showing that God puts His words in men's mouths, such as this one: "But the Lord said unto me, Say not, I am a child: for thou shalt go to all that I shall send thee, and whatsoever I command thee thou shalt speak. Be not afraid of their faces: for I am with thee to deliver thee, saith the Lord. Then the Lord put forth His hand, and touched my mouth. And the Lord said unto me, behold, I have put My words in thy mouth" (Jeremiah 1:7-9).

This scripture best depicts what I think happened to me. It felt as if I was speaking God's thoughts. Then, without hesitation, I heard the voice of God answer. He said, "My son, you have the gift of showing people how to love one another. As soon as I heard those words, I experienced deep understanding. I understood that the suffering I was going through was a blessing to my friends and family. This goes against man's understanding. Suffering is bad in any book, right? But as I began to read the scriptures, I found that godly suffering produces blessing. The apostle Paul wrote this: "Wherefore I desire that ye faint not at my tribulations for you, which is your glory" (Ephesians 3:13).

After hearing and understanding the meaning of these words, I replied, "God, if that is what my suffering will do for my loved ones, then let me suffer." I knew that God accepted these words, and I had a feeling I was really going to suffer. Looking back, that's the way it turned out. With that, I woke up and found myself sitting straight up in bed, crying and shaking as a flood of emotions filled my heart.

The next day, I had many questions that had been left unanswered. Did I really have a conversation with God? And if so, why would He take the time to speak to me? And why am I having all these strange dreams? What was going on? And by the way, who is God?

Many years later, I discovered that God has a special place where it is dark. That doesn't make much sense to me, because our God is a God of light. But in a dream, God told me to read this scripture: "He made darkness His 'secret place,' His pavilion round about Him were dark waters and thick clouds of the skies" (Psalm 18:11).

Recovering from my drug overdose took a while. I was laid up for a full month, as I recovered little by little. I quit my job, as I was no longer able to handle the intense pace it involved. That Angel Dust almost killed me and it slowed me down for some time. It took a while to heal but I finally began to feel confident enough to go back to work.

Not having a plan for the future and having little if any education, I got back into sales. This was not a good idea, because the rejection kept me in a constant state of anxiety. I went from one job to the next, trying to feel good about myself. I had no self-esteem, and each new job left me feeling more hopeless. I started drinking again to numb the pain as I forged ahead looking for a place of peace. It took a year of searching before I found a job that worked out for me.

I was 24 and tired of going from one job to the next. I heard through the grapevine that Sears was going to open a store in the Tacoma Mall, so off I went to apply for a position. I was hired and started a job that would be emotionally and financially rewarding.

I was making good money, working on commission in the television department. I moved into a one-bedroom house fifty feet from American Lake. It even had its own private dock. Life was starting to look pretty good. I had a new job and a great place by the water. With things going so well, I almost forgot my past sadness and I seldom thought about those unusual dreams. Although I was happy with my circumstances, I was living a life not pleasing to God. Deeply wounded, I was still trying to fill that empty spot in my heart with things that cannot satisfy. I was about to find out that God Himself was going to deal with me directly concerning one of the areas I needed to change.

I desperately needed to feel loved, and I was filling this need with things not pleasing to God. I was unable to see that I was destroying any hope of true joy by violating God's laws. Without godly direction from my earthly father, my heavenly Father decided to step in and correct my ways. The following encounter with God not only got my attention; it permanently changed the course of my life and forced me to make some dramatic changes in my behavior.

It was summer in Tacoma, and for me this meant lakeside barbecues, swimming, waterskiing, and long days spent basking in the sun. After swimming all day, I would go to bed early with hardly enough energy to make it past nine o'clock. One night while sleeping soundly, I found myself standing inside what seemed to be a huge courtroom. This was no ordinary place; everything was perfect. The floor was solid marble and so beautiful that words cannot do it justice. I looked to see a most unusual and beautiful sight. I knew I was in heaven.

The architecture was stunning. I looked in every direction to see buildings stretching as far as the eye could see. Each building was perfect in every way. Then I looked up. The ceiling of this timeless place was at least two thousand feet high. It seemingly went on forever, and I could not see far enough to reach the end. This was definitely not earth. The Bible says heaven is a place. I wasn't floating around on a cloud or playing a harp.

After that, a woman appeared out of thin air and was standing in front of me, about ten feet away. She appeared to be in her early 30s and looked normal in every way, except for the fact that she was undressed. Suddenly I became confused and wondered why I was standing in this heavenly hall facing this unusual woman.

I recall her standing at attention, like a military soldier stands when attending his post. I'm not sure if she was alive, because I did not see her move or blink or even breathe, for that matter. Then I heard God's powerful voice. He was speaking directly into my right ear.

"My son, this is lust. If you do not stop your sexual behavior, I will take away your ability to have sex for a while." Then the scene changed. I was no longer in the courtroom. I was now standing before what I knew to be a judgment throne. It looked as if it had been there forever. I remember thinking that it had an eternal look to it. This throne seemed at least two hundred feet high and made of a solid piece of beautiful white marble. On either side of this majestic structure were pillars and Roman-style buildings.

Here is a picture of that beautiful place:

Covering the top of this fantastic structure was a boiling cloud that seemed to be intelligently controlled. Lightning was flashing all around and I somehow knew that God's presence was just behind this impenetrable covering.

This pillar was about two hundred feet tall and made out of solid marble. It was pure white and it sparkled with Heavenly perfection. I was standing before the "Great-White-Throne" we read about in the book of Revelation!

Artistic rendition of the Great-White-Throne that I stood before in my second vision from God!

I could not see the top of the throne, because a dark cloud covered the top portion. Thick clouds swirled around the top of this monolith, and powerful lightning bolts were bursting in all directions. Instantly I knew that beyond my vision and behind the powerful clouds sat the Judge, God Himself, and I understood that I would not be allowed to see His face. I also understood that I was there for one reason and one reason only: to be judged and receive a penalty for my sins.

After realizing this, I looked down and saw my body naked before God. I was totally exposed, both physically and spiritually. Then I saw a horrible sight—little black snakes clinging to my private parts and my thighs! Their bites felt like bee stings, and I started screaming with all that was in me. I awoke in terror and confusion. This dream seemed so real; I knew this was no ordinary event.

Well, I don't think I have to tell you that this shook me up. I was more than scared. I remembered the last two dreams and what happened shortly after each one. I knew God had just given me a warning. I was so upset I drove over to my parents' house to share what had just happened. Not being Christians at the time, they passed this off as just another dream formed by a wild imagination. I knew better this time, and I decided to change my ways. I wanted nothing to do with those little black snakes.

I wasn't sure which end was up. If God was real, then how should I be living my life? I had a million unanswered questions. It had not yet dawned on me to go to church and find out what God had to say about life. Using my own intellect, I devised a plan to keep myself from sinning. With a lot of confidence, I looked forward to a life free from error. But the Bible says that "the spirit is willing, but the flesh is weak." I found out that my flesh was no exception.

About a month after having this disturbing dream I received a call from the mother of my high school sweetheart. She asked if I could help her daughter heal from a painful divorce. She said her daughter caught her husband cheating on her, and it broke her heart. She added that I was the only man her daughter trusted, and she wanted me to call her to see if I could cheer her up.

So I made the call and found myself sitting in a coffee shop with my ex, talking about life and its pains and sorrows. A familiar attraction was starting to stir in my heart. This was the one person in my past that I regretted leaving. I should have married her, but we were so young, and life seemed to be calling me to stay single. So we had gone our separate ways. I went off to find myself, and she ended up getting married a few years later.

Now we were sitting in this café, and the sparks were really flying. Before I knew it we were holding each other and doing the one thing I had promised God I would not do. The Bible states in many places that the flesh is truly weak. Looking back, I can testify to that truth, and I feel perplexed at the depth of my foolishness. Here I was, not thirty days after receiving God's warning, and I was doing the very thing I promised I would never do again. Oh, wretched man that I am; who can deliver me from this body of sin?

Later that night I awoke feeling troubled. How could I break my promise so easily? I had purposely forgotten my promise and looked the other way. But God will not be mocked, and His words will not return unto Him void. Two days later it became obvious that something was wrong. I felt as if I had the flu, and I noticed something wrong with my skin. I went to the doctor, and after a quick examination, he pronounced his findings. It turns out that I contracted the herpes virus. I had the classic symptoms.

The news shocked me. Along with the knowledge that I now had an incurable disease, I realized that I truly had heard from God. That dream wasn't the product of an over-active imagination. I had been in God's presence, and He had warned me and then judged me. This reality shook me to the core of my being.

Broken and confounded, I accepted this sentence. I had gotten exactly what I deserved. One thing is certain—God was real, and He was speaking to me. From this point on I decided to actively search until I found out who God really was. I became determined to find out what He wanted from me and what I should do about that. Looking back, I realize I had no clue that He was going to show me extraordinary things and that He had a specific purpose in showing me these things.

The Bible says, "The Lord is gracious and compassionate, slow to anger, and rich in love" (Psalm 145:8). Many people asked, "If God is so loving, then why all the rules? And if He loves you, why did He give you that awful disease?" Having been a Christian for many years, I have learned much through mistakes and experiences. I have asked these same questions, and God has been faithful to show me the answers.

First of all, God gave the law to protect us, not to inhibit us. The Bible says, "For the wages of sin is death; but the free gift of God is eternal life in Christ Jesus our Lord" (Romans 6:23). God knows the consequences of sin. If you receive Jesus as Lord and Savior you will go to heaven. But God never said that you would not suffer the consequences of your ways. In fact, the book of Galatians says, "Be not deceived; God is not mocked: for whatsoever a man soweth, that shall he also reap" (Galatians 6:7). I am a living picture of this fact. I am born again, bought and paid for by the precious blood of Jesus, and yet this virus affects my life to this day.

Secondly, God did not want me to have herpes. He tried to warn me, and I did not listen. In similar fashion, His Word warns us that without Jesus, we will be going to eternal judgment. How about you? Will you listen to God's warning? Will you receive forgiveness for your sins, or will you let your pride and foolishness keep you from the gates of heaven?

Thirdly, having the herpes virus has been a grievous thing. I have shed many tears over my past actions. But it has also been a blessing. I will even go as far as to say that I see God loving me by allowing me to suffer the consequences of my sinful ways. This virus has shown me in a dynamic way that sin does indeed produce death. I have learned how precious our bodies are and I now know that our health is a gift from God and is to be preserved at all cost.

Finally, it has been a constant reminder that other more harmful things could happen if I continue breaking God's laws. I know this all too well. In May of 1995 I attended my biological father's funeral. He died of complications from AIDS and went to his grave denying Jesus Christ. So I thank God He loved me enough to compel me to put a stop to my sinful ways.

♦ 3 ♦

Coming to Jesus

⌒

For me, coming to Jesus was as natural as a fish swimming in water. After three encounters with the Lord, I was already convinced God was real. All that was left to do was go to church and hear the gospel. The Bible says faith comes by hearing and hearing from the Word of God. I had never heard the words of God, so naturally I had no faith. Two years would pass before the Lord would draw me into His kingdom.

Still working at Sears, I went about my business as I always had. I seemed the same on the outside, but inside I was going through many changes. I tried to make sense out of life and understand its purpose. Two coworkers, Fred and Leon, kept reminding me that I needed to go to church to discover the meaning of life. Leon told me about this wonderful church he attended known as Life Center. I knew they were right about church, but I was afraid. After all, none of my friends went to church, and I thought they would reject me if I went. I found out later that these are normal feelings when a man chooses between the ways of the world and the ways of God.

Not having a Christian friend at the time, I was on my own in deciding whether to attend church. This may sound easy, but I was afraid to go. I kept putting it off. A year went by, and I had all but abandoned my plan to go.

That year for me was one of sadness. Joy had all but left me. The things I once liked to do were no longer satisfying. Herpes constantly caused me physical problems, and I felt guilty over my past behavior. Parties became stressful and left me feeling empty and confused. I knew I needed to change, but I kept going in circles. Looking back, I can see God using these failures to get me ready to receive the truth. The Bible says, "But we are bound to give thanks to God always for you, brethren beloved by the Lord, because God chose you from the beginning to be saved, through sanctification by the spirit and belief in the truth. To this he called you through our gospel, so that you may obtain the glory of our Lord Jesus Christ" (2 Thessalonians 2:13-14).

Not knowing this at the time, I felt as if life was nothing but sorrow. I felt no reason to continue living a life that had no real purpose. I was to find out later that God had chosen me and was drawing me to Him. This was going to give me every reason to live!

With so many worries on my heart, I became restless and decided to look for a new job. I liked working at Sears, but I was a part-time employee and was told that in the future most of the employees would be part time. Not satisfied with that, I accepted a job working for Bon Marché. They needed someone to work in the TV department, and with lots of experience in that area, I naturally got the job. It was June, and living on American Lake made working the last thing on my priority list so I arranged to take a month off for a much-needed rest. It was during this month that the Lord would start giving me dreams of the coming destruction.

One night in a dream, I found myself standing just outside the heart of New York City. It was night, and it must have been summer because it was comfortably warm and I was not wearing a jacket of any kind. It was a beautiful night. I was enjoying watching the lights of this majestic city. New York is truly amazing and as I scanned the horizon I noticed a bright light coming down out of the sky. It was white and looked like a large flare. It was about two thousand feet above the buildings in the center of the city. I noticed that it looked as if it was attached to a parachute, because it was drifting down slowly, and the flare-like light was rocking back and forth from the force of the wind.

All of a sudden it happened. From just above the spot where the flare was drifting came an explosion that engulfed the city. It was either an atomic or a hydrogen bomb. All I could see was a blinding light. My eyes had automatically closed, but I was still able to see the force of the blast move through the city like a tidal wave. I could feel the heat as the power of this bomb advanced through the city, burning everything to the ground. In seconds it reached the place where I was standing, and I was jolted out of my sleep as the power of the bomb engulfed me.

I lay in bed thinking that these dreams were somehow going to change the course of my life. Could this be a true vision of the destruction of New York? If New York is going to be destroyed by an atomic bomb, who was going to do this, and why? I suddenly felt the need to get to God as soon as possible.

It was a week before I was to start my new job, and I began to prepare myself mentally for the stress that a new job would bring. Having a confidence problem made change of any kind difficult, so I was nervous about my first day on the job. This kept my mind off the dreams and on more immediate matters. Then I had another vision of future events.

In this dream I found myself looking out the window of the second story of an apartment building. The window was open, and I was leaning out, looking at the scene below. It was dark outside, and yet, I somehow knew that it was day.

As I looked out over the landscape, everything in my field of vision was destroyed by a huge explosion.

The buildings were leveled; the grass and the trees were burned up. Destruction was everywhere. An enemy tank rolled over the rubble and seeing no visible markings I didn't know which country the tank belonged to. There was a wind in the air that seemed to be alive and I could feel spiritual energy in the air.

Then I felt fear rise up inside my spirit. It felt as if something bad was about to happen to me. All of a sudden the window started to slam back and forth without anyone touching it. I was terrified. I turned to see all the furniture moving by demon power. I began choking as if a huge hand had seized my throat—I mean for real! I couldn't breathe and began gasping for air. I thought I was going to die right then. I cried out, "God, help me!" And just as suddenly as this dream started, it stopped.

I immediately sat up with my stomach tied in knots. I was nauseous, and fear gripped my mind. I cried out to God to find out why these things were happening to me. The choking was real. It wasn't my imagination. After this incident I knew beyond question that spirits and demons were real. From that day on I had a fearful respect for the things of the spirit world. Looking back, I was unaware that I was going to have many future encounters with demons, including a few personal visits from Satan. I thank God that I didn't know that at the time, because encounters with evil spirits are disturbing, and I had little or no biblical understanding of this subject.

The Bible talks about a Day of Judgment: "Blow ye the trumpet in Zion, and sound an alarm in my holy mountain; let all the inhabitants of the land tremble: for the day of Jehovah cometh, for it is nigh at hand; a day of darkness and gloominess, a day of clouds and thick darkness, as the dawn spread upon the mountains; a great people and a strong; there hath not been ever the like, neither shall be any more after them, even to the years of many generations. A fire devoureth before them; and behind them a flame burneth: the land is as the Garden of Eden before them, and behind them a desolate wilderness; yea, and none hath escaped them" (Joel 2:2-3).

Had I been given a glimpse of that day? Since then I have talked with many people who have seen New York destroyed by nuclear fire. Many people have also seen the day of destruction in visions. In 1929 a man named A.C. Valdez had an open vision of intercontinental ballistic missiles (ICBMs) striking California as a judgment from God. He saw the vast California freeway systems we have today, and he saw the actual missiles that destroyed the region. Remember, in 1929 there was no freeway system, and the atomic bomb would not be developed until 1945. ICBMs were far in the future.

I am not writing this to scare anyone, but that day is going to come in the near future. God has made that as plain as day to me. Only those who enter into the Rock that is Christ Jesus will be saved. God is going to judge the earth, but He said this about His own people: "In an acceptable time have I heard thee, and in a day of salvation have I helped thee: and I will preserve thee, and give thee for a covenant of the people, to establish the earth, to cause to inherit the desolate heritage" (Isaiah 49:8). And from the New Testament, I found this scripture: "And I heard another voice from heaven, saying, Come out of her, My people, that ye be not partakers of her sins, and that ye receive not of her plagues" (Revelation 18:4). God's people will be protected from His wrath. My question to you is this: Are you going to be in the camp of the Lord or not?

After having this last dream my heart was full of questions. I knew these dreams were messages from heaven but I didn't know what to do about them. I was about to start a new job so I chose not to think about the dreams and focused on starting my new career.

Starting my new job was easier than I expected. In no time flat I was selling away and doing fine. There were some real characters in that place. The Bon people thought they were better than the common people, so I had a hard time fitting in.

One day as I was going to get some change for the register, I was stopped by two separate people who asked the same question: They both asked me if I was a Christian. At that time I still did not know what being a Christian meant. I knew I wanted to be one, though, and I asked them what being a Christian actually meant. Neither one of them had time to explain, so off we went to our workstations.

That day two more people asked me the same question. What was going on? I was 25 years old, and in my entire life only one person had asked me that question. Now, in one day, four people asked if I was a Christian. I had this feeling deep down inside that something supernatural was happening. God was knocking at my door, and I was about to open it and let Him in.

That same day a coworker, Scott Miller, started talking about me to people in the store. A couple of them told me what he had been saying. That made me mad, because what he had said wasn't true in any. Even though it was my first week on the job, I decided to confront him about this matter. Before we talked I noticed a "700 Club" button on his jacket. I knew about the 700 Club, and having that button on his jacket could only mean one thing: This guy was a Christian!

At this point I knew God was up to something. This was no ordinary day. Looking back it was this discussion with Scott that would eventually get me to church. It all turned out for God's glory, so today he and I can look back with awe at how the Lord worked in such a mysterious way.

I started this conversation with a question. I said, "If you are a Christian, and Christians are supposed to be so good, then why are you going around saying bad things about someone you don't even know?" This was my first week on the job, and we were just getting to know one another. I then repeated what he had said about me and pointed out the people who had told me.

With that he turned three shades of red. He was speechless. He probably thought that no one would say a thing. I thank God this happened, because after he apologized, we had a long talk about God. That started a great relationship that continues to this very day. Right after that, he told me he went to this great church—Life Center. When he asked me if I would like to go, it was crystal clear that God was calling me to this particular church. Knowing this was God calling, I accepted Scott's invitation, and we made plans to attend the next Sunday.

Life Center turned out to be a great blessing. Fulton Buntain is the pastor, a great teacher, and a fine man. At first I must have looked like an over-starched shirt as I listened to this man preach about Jesus. I was scared and felt totally out of place. But something started to happen. It was like a whisper at first. I could hear the truth behind the words as the gospel beckoned me. My heart started to warm as I discovered for the first time that life actually had meaning.

Then the pastor told us that God is our true Father. He said He would never leave me, and He wanted to take me in His arms and hold me forever! I already knew God was real, because I had heard His voice and felt His presence in the dreams He had given me. What I lacked was a full understanding of His love for me. To think that He loved me so much that He sent His only Son, Jesus, to die a horrible death so I might go to heaven! This broke me to the center of my being.

My earthly father had left us after years of control and abuse, so when the pastor said God would never leave me nor forsake me, I was deeply moved. I felt those words tugging on my heart like a warm fire on a winter's night. I could not resist His love anymore, so I rushed to the altar at the end of the service and received Jesus as my Lord and Savior. That was the turning point in my life. I thank God that He called me to be with Him in a place called heaven, where time has no hold on us and sickness is not even listed in the dictionary.

♦ 4 ♦

God Calls Again

A fter I received Jesus, I left my job at the Bon to take an outside sales job. This job entailed selling gold chain and diamonds to jewelry stores in the Pacific Northwest, which meant I was able to listen to Christian radio for hours at a time as I drove around the region. I learned a lot about the ways of God listening to sermon after sermon on the radio. I remember hanging on every word as I amassed a treasure of scriptures to get me through my stressful days.

One night at a hotel, God gave me a dream that was both a promise and a picture of my walk with Him. I found myself standing at the top of a perfectly round crater in the ground. The top of this crater was about the size of a football field, and the sides were gently sloped so that a person could go down the hill without much danger of falling. The slopes were covered with the most beautiful, perfect grass I had ever seen. Every blade was exactly the same in color and thickness. Even the way they pointed was perfect.

At the bottom of the crater, I saw a pond made of liquid crystal. It looked to be about forty feet in diameter. I knew this pond was not of this earth. It was so strikingly beautiful that I heard myself groan within. It was the most unusual color I had ever seen, a light blue like an aquamarine, and it had an intensity that reminded me of neon. It was sparkling clean like a precious stone, and it was so clear you could see down forever. I remember feeling as if I was looking into eternity. It almost seemed as if the pond was a window, and on the other side was a place where time did not exist.

As I looked on, my eyes began to see something coming up from the depths, from the other side of the glass-smooth surface of this crystal pond. It was a fish of some sort that floated closer and closer to the top and stopped just below the surface of the pond. All through this vision, the surface of the pond remained as smooth as glass. The fish was lying motionless on its side, and I knew it was letting me get a good look at it. It was shaped like a salmon and had olive green skin and silver scales with the colors of the rainbow mixed in. This was no ordinary fish! The colors sparkled, making a wonderful sight.

After about ten seconds the fish gently rolled over to an upright position. I felt as if I had been granted a certain amount of time to view this magnificent sight, and my time was now up. As the fish rolled over, its tail gently swept in a half-circle motion. This motion was so smooth that it did not break the surface of the pond. It looked like poetry in motion. As the fish moved, I received a message in something like sign language, but instead of human hands making the motions, it was a fish's tail. I knew who was sending the message to me—it was Jesus. He said: "Come, and I will give you total peace, total rest."

Jesus said: "Peace I leave with you; My peace I give unto you: not as the world giveth, give I unto you. Let not your heart be troubled, neither let it be fearful" (John 14:27). The Bible also makes many statements about entering His rest, including this one that comes closest to what He was saying in this vision: "There remaineth therefore a Sabbath rest for the people of God" (Hebrews 4:9). God said we should work six days and on the seventh day, God's day, we should rest.

The Bible teaches there is a Sabbath-day rest for the children of God, one that will last forever. Jesus was saying in this vision that I too would enter into that rest through the sacrificial blood that Jesus shed on the cross two thousand years ago.

Years later, I came upon this confirming scripture: "And before the throne, as it were a sea of glass like a crystal, and in the midst of the throne, and round about the throne, four living creatures full of eyes before and behind" (Revelation 4:6). Could this be a heavenly glimpse into eternity?

Longing to receive what had just been promised, I bolted down the hill with everything in my heart crying, "Yes, Lord Jesus, I will come." When I got to the bottom, the scene changed. In a twinkling of an eye I was standing before an awesome sight. Before me was a raging river, a torrent of churning water that was boiling above ground. That seemed impossible, but it was churning up to the height of my neck. I'm five foot six, so the water was boiling up five feet above level ground.

I noticed the magnificent fish in the midst of the churning waves. It was going down river as the powerful waves moved it along. I knew that if I didn't jump in, I would lose sight of the fish. I was terrified at the thought of jumping in because it was so rough, but I knew I had to do it. I leaned forward to jump but was thrown out of the dream due to fear.

I sat straight up with my heart racing and my breathing fast and labored, as if I had just run a long-distance race. I was deeply moved because I knew I had just seen Jesus, in a most unusual way. I wasn't sure if I had jumped in the river, so I asked the Lord to strengthen my heart to follow Him.

Looking back I can truly say that I did jump in. I found out by experience that a walk with the Lord is a difficult thing. That churning water was a picture of a life lived for Christ. The Bible says: "Yea, and all that would live godly lives in Christ Jesus shall suffer persecution" (2 Timothy

3:12). But we shouldn't lose hope, because the Word of God also promises that in the end those who have served Him will enter an eternal reward. You will receive the reward of your faith, the salvation of your souls: "Receiving the end of your faith, even the salvation of your souls" (1 Peter 1:9).

Shortly after this dream, the complexion of my life began to change. The company that paid me so well was now in financial trouble and filed for bankruptcy. My two-year relationship with my girlfriend ended, and sudden unemployment left me with little choice but to move in with the one person who would never leave me nor forsake me—my mother.

This was the start of what I would call a wilderness journey. In the four seasons analogy, this would be winter, and in this case it was going to be a record breaker. That raging water turned out to be a prophetic picture of the painful affliction I was about to go through.

Staying with my parents turned out to be rather nice. We got to know each other again, and I had some time to reflect on my future. Having thought about my true goals in life I decided to apply for a job with a utilities company. I knew utilities would always be needed and would be unaffected by economic slumps. It took four months of filling out applications, but I finally got a job with Washington Natural Gas.

Starting from day one, my new job was a painful experience that I wish I could forget. The ten-week training course almost did me in. Right from the start I had problems with the people in my class. The class became a platform for each student to make his mark as a go-getter. This is typical in sales-oriented jobs. The motto is always the same: "Winning isn't everything; it's the only thing!" Needless to say, having low self-esteem made this difficult for me. For ten weeks I cried every night and felt oppressed every day.

The pressure was so great that it nearly broke my spirit. I was an outcast; the people in the class would have nothing to do with me. I asked God many times why I was made to suffer like this, and I got no answer. My parents suffered as well. I would come home looking as if I was ready for the grave. They wondered why God let this happen to someone who put his trust in Him. I prayed daily for an answer but got none. It took several weeks of prayer before God would start to show me why I was there.

It was now two weeks until graduation, and we had learned more about heating homes than one can imagine. The last two weeks we were going out in the field to look at different jobs and to review what we had learned in the classroom. We piled into one of the company vehicles, and off we went.

On our way to a work site, we got behind a car that had a Christian fish symbol on the bumper. One of the guys in the class started yelling, "Look, it's one of those Christian idiots!" Following their hero and leader, my classmates all started saying things about God and His children that I can't and won't repeat. They all knew I was a Christian, and I'm pretty sure they did this to hurt my feelings.

Then God spoke to my heart. I did not hear His voice, but I knew His thoughts. These scriptures came to my heart: "Blessed are ye, when men shall hate you, and when they shall separate you from their company, and reproach you, and cast out your name as evil, for the Son of man's sake" (Luke 6:22). This scripture became real to me; these people would not even eat with me during lunch breaks. If I sat on the right side of the lunchroom, they would sit on the left, and that is how it went through the entire training.

I found another revealing passage spoken by Jesus. He proclaimed; "If the world hateth you, ye know that it hath hated me before it hated you" (John 15:18).

This was my first practical lesson in suffering for Jesus. After the Lord gave me those two scriptures, I had a bit more peace. I went around telling myself that "this too shall pass." This little saying helped me through the rest of the training.

Upon graduation, I wanted nothing to do with natural gas or the company that controlled it. My heart was gripped with fear because I was unsure I could do the job. I had been so stressed out in the classroom that I forgot most of what I needed to know so I avoided getting a territory of my own. While the rest of my classmates were competing for a chance to get out and make the big bucks, I was retreating into the break room to hide my shame.

The Bible says that not even a sparrow falls to the ground without God's knowledge, so my situation was no surprise to God. Scripture also says that those who put their trust in God will not be ashamed. What I didn't know was that God was going to turn the tables on the situation, and I was going to make a bold statement for Him.

It was no secret that I wasn't gung-ho for natural gas. The instructor was definitely not a Christian, and during our field training some things happened that were disgusting at best. So I didn't care what the company thought of me, I just wanted out.

It happened that one of the women who sold gas ranges and barbecues was pregnant. She was going on maternity leave, and the company needed someone to take her place. This was a starting position for gas sales reps and was looked down on as a loser job by the outside salespeople. They needed to fill this position, however, and guess who was chosen to take over the position. Me! So off I went to Seattle to start my new job selling gas appliances on the showroom floor.

This turned out to be a blessing. I had years of retail selling experience, and I had just come through the most thorough training you can imagine. This helped me sell something to just about everyone who came in to ask about gas products. Other duties were to answer customer questions by phone and make appointments for the outside salespeople. This was easy and enjoyable work. In our area, natural gas is considerably cheaper than electricity, and it has always been more efficient. So I spent my day rattling off interesting facts to people who had called about switching from electricity to gas.

The days began to fly by. I actually liked my new position, but I knew my days were numbered. The woman I was filling in for was only going to be gone three months, and then I would be forced into getting a territory. The thought of this was unbearable, so I began looking for a new job right away. As it turned out, Steve Johnson, a friend who worked for a national publishing firm, called and asked if I would like a job working in the magazine industry. Thanking God for my deliverance, I accepted the new position, which was to start in a month.

Just before I turned in my two-week notice, one of the bosses came out on the showroom floor. He told me he wanted to talk to me in his office. I thought I had done something wrong. *I can't wait to get out of here,* I thought.

He stopped just outside his office. Then all the sales reps came into the room, and I mean all of them. It was quite a show of people, and it included the people I went through training with. They were all looking at me as I stood there wondering what this was all about. Then the manager started to speak and, much to my surprise, it wasn't a rebuke at all. He started commending me on a job well done. He read aloud from customer-remark cards as the sales crew looked on. Customers had written in to thank me for taking the time to tell them about natural gas and its benefits.

He then said that the outside sales reps were discovering that customers were already sold on switching to gas. He said this unusual success was a result of my explanations over the phone and that this had never happened before — ever! The strange thing was the hateful looks on the faces of those I trained with. They didn't like this at all. I just stood there thanking God for helping me triumph in the midst of a hopeless situation.

A week later, God delivered me from this awful place. My high school friend "Steve Johnson" called and asked me if I would be willing to accept a job with his employer. He worked for a publishing company and they needed a man to take the Eastern Washington territory.

I accepted his offer and one week later I turned in my two-week notice. This shook things up at the gas company, because no one had ever quit this position that I know of. The president of the company came to the showroom the next day to ask me why I was leaving. I told him what had happened in the training class and gave him some feedback about changes that needed to take place for the salespeople to stay motivated. (I learned about these problems while riding with the long-time sales reps.) Later, I heard that the sales department went through some positive changes due to the talk I had with him. I also found out that most of the people in my training class got fired or quit shortly thereafter. I couldn't believe I had gone through so much misery for what seemed to end up equaling a big zero.

Looking back, however, I see God showing me how foolish it was to strive after the things the world holds so dear. I tried so hard to be something that I couldn't and shouldn't be. I started having panic attacks that left me feeling hopeless and scared. My heart pounded out of control as I tried to prepare myself for the new job I was about to start.

Starting my new career as a publisher's rep was a drain on what little life I had left in me. For one thing, I had to move to Spokane to take over an abandoned territory. I had never lived in an unfamiliar city before, and I was terrified. With my confidence level close to zero, I fought to keep myself together long enough to learn this new job.

The first day on the job went well. It was ninety-five degrees in Spokane, and the blue sky helped me to think positive thoughts as I drove to meet my new boss. I was nervous and apprehensive after my experience at the gas company, but after five minutes with my new boss, Bill Dahlgren, I could sense that I was safe, so I relaxed and tried to enjoy the day.

That day we had lunch and went over my job description. Bill took me down to meet the local wholesaler, and with our initial introduction out of the way, we went to my apartment to set up a filing system that would keep me organized. I sensed that Bill was a kind and loving man. He was patient with me, and it wasn't long before I felt led to ask him if he was a Christian. (This is taboo in the business world, but I mentioned the Lord as often as I felt led, and it never once caused trouble.) I tensely waited for an answer. To my joy and relief he responded with a resounding "Yes!"

This started a beautiful friendship that has lasted to this very day. God had brought us together for a lot of reasons. Some I will write about later in this book, but for now He was using Bill to help me get the job done.

Spokane turned out to be a nice city. The weather is warm in the summer, and I enjoyed the blue sky and gorgeous sunsets. The only problem was that I had no friends there. I was alone in a new city and couldn't find anyone to spend my time with. I ate alone, went shopping alone, and spent my weekends alone.

I tried to meet people, but that was difficult because I traveled for a living and spent my weekdays in other cities. I would drag myself home late Friday afternoon and be on the road again Monday morning. This was very hard on me, and it took a toll on my physical strength.

That is when God began to deal with me about the meaning of life. I had a lot of time to reflect on the reasons we do things. I had a house full of beautiful things, and that seemed well and good, but it didn't make me feel satisfied. To keep from feeling lonely I began to spend my weekends searching for the perfect piece of art to match my perfect little apartment. The place was beautiful, but I was angry. I had all this stuff, but nobody came over to see it. It felt as if I had a shield around me that kept people away. I got to the point of starting to hate the things I had acquired. I was killing myself daily to pay for stuff that nobody ever saw. What a tragic and lonely existence!

I began to slip into a depression that came on so slowly I didn't even know I was in trouble. I started drinking wine just about every night to kill the pain. To get through my lonely weekends, I would rent movies to keep me company and drink wine to keep me numb. In between, I broke down and cried a lot.

The one thing I did have in my favor was a relationship with God. I was a baby Christian in every sense of the word. I rarely read the Bible, and I had a limited understanding of the Word. I did know I was saved, however, and I knew God had spoken to me in those unusual dreams.

God had me right where He wanted me. He was about to start moving in my life in a big way, and I realized He was directing and leading me in the way that I should go. He was using the failures and stress that came with my jobs to strip my heart of foolish desires. At the same time He was replacing them with the desire to serve Him. He was making all things work together for my good, and I came to a place of total submission to His will. With that accomplished, He could now start showing me the things He wanted me to see, and show me He did!

One night in my little apartment in Spokane, I was watching a movie and drinking wine in my usual battle against loneliness and boredom. This was typical for a Saturday night, but this night was going to turn out to be anything but typical. I couldn't focus on the plot of the movie, so I shut it off and began flipping the channels to see what might be on. I came across TBN, a Christian station. A man on the screen was carrying a large cross, and a lot of people were gathering around him. I turned up the volume and started watching what was going on.

As he began to preach, my heart began to melt. He talked about how futile and foolish it was to not live for Jesus. Those words were powerful; I had wasted my life on the pursuit of personal possessions and glory. I was the guy he was preaching about. Then I looked around my place and felt ashamed. I had spent hundreds of dollars on things that didn't matter. Not only that, I also had to go through extreme stress and abuse to get these things.

It all seemed so foolish. I was moved to the center of my soul, and I cried out loud to my possessions, "I sold my soul for you, and in return I got nothing!" What a strange thing to do! But I was angry at myself for being deceived into living this way.

I then turned my attention back to the man on TV. As I watched, I noticed how the people seemed to be attracted to the cross. They were crying and falling down before the cross, and I knew I was watching something supernatural taking place. A question popped into my mind. I said to God, "I know why Jesus had to die for our salvation, but of all the ways a man can be put to death, You must have had a special reason to pick the cross. That cross must represent something special—what is it?"

In the twinkling of an eye an alarm went off in my spirit. I heard these words: "Quick, get your Bible, and I'll show you in my Word!" Those were the exact words I heard, and I leaped out of my chair and ran to my bedroom to get my Bible. I prayed for God to show me what the cross of Christ represented. With that I closed my eyes and randomly opened the Bible.

My eyes fell on these words: "The word of Jehovah came again unto me, saying, And thou, son of man, take thee one stick, and write upon it, For Judah, and for the children of Israel his companions: then take another stick, and write upon it, For Joseph, the stick of Ephraim, and for all the house of Israel his companions: and join them for thee one to another into one stick, that they may become one in thy hand. And when the children of thy people shall speak unto thee, saying, Wilt thou not show us what thou meanest by these? say unto them, Thus saith the Lord Jehovah: Behold, I will take the stick of Joseph, which is in the hand of Ephraim, and the tribes of Israel his companions; and I will put them with it, even with the stick of Judah, and make them one stick, and they shall be one in my hand" (Ezekiel 37:16-19).

I could hardly believe my eyes. I saw the cross in my mind. It is actually two pieces of wood. Could this be from God? Is this what the cross represents, two people becoming one?

Before I could finish thinking these thoughts, God spoke audibly to me, saying, "My son, are you willing to sell all that you have and follow Me?"

I cried out, "Yes, yes, Lord, I am willing!" I burst out crying and was shaking all over. I was overwhelmed that God had just spoken to me audibly. He was calling me to live the rest of my life for Him and not myself. It was going to be a total change of lifestyle, and I felt that God had heard my response and had accepted me for His purpose. The Bible says, "For many are called, but few are chosen" (Matthew 22:14). I went to sleep knowing God had chosen me for some kind of ministry.

Years later, I came across this scripture. "But now in Christ Jesus ye that once were far off are made nigh in the blood of Christ. For he is our peace, who made both one, and broke down the middle wall of partition, having abolished in the flesh the enmity, even the law of commandments contained in ordinances; that He might create in Himself of the two one new man, so making peace; and might reconcile them both in one body unto God through the cross, having slain the enmity thereby" (Ephesians 2:14-16).

What an awesome God we serve. I thank God that He chose me, a foolish man whose weakness was evident in the way he lived his life. Why God would have anything to do with me was a mystery. The night He asked me to serve Him, I was drunk. I heard His voice and felt His powerful presence. Why God would have anything to do with a man like me is beyond my comprehension.

Then I came across this passage in my Bible: "But God chose the foolish things of the world, that he might put to shame them that are wise; and God chose the weak things of the world, that he might put to shame the things that are strong" (1 Corinthians 1:27). Looking back, I can now see the beauty in the way God chooses.

♦ 5 ♦

The Holy Spirit a Reality

The Bible was given to us for many reasons. It gives us guidelines for living and a history of our faith. It gives us a picture of our heavenly Father, His Son Jesus, and His precious Holy Spirit, sent to be our constant companion and friend. From the beginning of the scriptures to the end, it is chock-full of information on the works and nature of our God.

Not knowing God's Word fully, I had a limited understanding of His ways. Except for the few times God had spoken to me, I thought He spoke only to His holy priests and then only in special circumstances or in times of prophetic importance. What I didn't know is that God speaks to common people like me and that we are living in times of critical prophetic importance. God's Word says: "And it shall come to pass afterward, that I will pour out my Spirit upon all flesh; and your sons and your daughters shall prophesy, your old men shall dream dreams, your young men shall see visions" (Joel 2:28).

I was confused about God's methods of choosing people. I thought He chose the tallest, smartest, most popular, and best-looking people, those who were raised in perfect families, read the Bible, and prayed continually. What I found out through experience is that God sometimes picks the least likely person to be His messenger. The Bible puts it this way: "But God chose the foolish things of the world, that he might put to shame them that are wise; and God chose the weak things of the world, that he might put to shame the things that are strong. and the base things of the world, and the things that are despised, did God choose, yea and the things that are not, that He might bring to naught the things that are: that no flesh should glory before God" (1 Corinthians 1:27-29).

Jesus gave us a beautiful picture of this truth when He chose twelve men to be His special ambassadors. He called these men "apostles." He bypassed the religious men of that day and chose fishermen, a tax collector, and common men for this special ministry. Before sending them out, He equipped them for service by giving them the Holy Spirit. This gave them the power to cast out demons, heal the sick, and boldly preach the gospel of Jesus Christ.

I was to find out later that God had chosen me to preach the gospel, but before I could do this I would need to receive that same power through the baptism of the Holy Spirit. Not understanding all that, I went about my business as usual. Little did I know God had already prepared the time and place where He would first pour out this precious gift on me. He had it all arranged and chose my next visit to Tacoma to be the acceptable time. Here is how it all happened.

Having no friends in Spokane left me lonely and bored. My dull weekends left me feeling empty and sad. I became desperate for company, and decided to pack my bags and head for home. I missed my friends and family and didn't mind the 6-hour drive that brought me back home.

Little did I know, this visit to Tacoma was actually appointed by God. He was going to make good His promise to fill me with His Spirit and this event was going to turn my heart in a new direction. Receiving God's Spirit was going to change my heart forever, and set the course of my life on fire—Holy Spirit fire!

I was totally unaware of God's plans as I entered the city limits of Tacoma. I was focused on relaxing around the kitchen table with my folks and finding out how the family was doing. It was 4 p.m., and I decided to stop by and see my friend, Nick Sakellis, who worked in the carpet department at Sears. This would only take a few minutes out of my trip, because Sears was near the freeway that led to my parents' home.

Nick greeted me with a great big smile and a huge hug. He was surprised to see me and asked me what I was doing in Tacoma. We made small talk for a few minutes. Then we began discussing the things of God. I told him how God had spoken to me audibly and had asked if I would sell all to follow Him. He was greatly encouraged and said he also had something to share with me.

He told me about a woman named Tillie who had seen many miracles in her life. She had even written a book about some of the things God had done for her. She was having a meeting that night at her house and had invited him to come and hear a man from Africa preach and pray in the power of the Holy Ghost. I didn't know what that power was all about, but I felt God wanted me to go so I accepted his offer and changed my plans for the evening.

We arrived half an hour early, and Tillie greeted us at the front door. She was a very straightforward person, and she helped me relax as we waited for this man from Africa to give us the Word of God. The house began to fill up, and I began thinking that this man must be something special for all these people to cram into Tillie's house.

Because we had arrived early, we had good seats on the front room couch. As we sat there I heard some women on the second-story balcony speaking in an unfamiliar language. I thought they must have been praying, because they had their arms raised with their eyes closed. They were speaking in what sounded like broken syllables. I had never seen or heard, such a sight. Nick looked at me, and I knew he was thinking the same thing.

Finally this young African man came up from the downstairs bedroom. He was a handsome black fellow, and I guessed him to be about 25 years old. He introduced himself as Emmanuel and gave a brief testimony about God calling him into the ministry and sending him to America.

He began preaching about the power of God. He said God had baptized him in the Holy Spirit, and he offered many scriptures that convinced us that God indeed wanted to pour out His Spirit on all who believe.

The atmosphere of the night changed. Emmanuel started to call up one person at a time and pray for them. This was the first time I had ever seen this done, and one person after another broke down crying as God ministered to them. These people looked shocked as the secrets of their hearts were made bare for healing. The Bible puts it this way: "But if all prophesy, and there come in one unbelieving or unlearned, he is reproved by all, he is judged by all; the secrets of his heart are made manifest; and so he will fall down on his face and worship God, declaring that God is among you indeed" (1 Corinthians 14:24-25). This man was prophesying through the power of God's Spirit, and we all could see that this was the real thing. At this point Nick and I were stunned and speechless. We looked at each other in awe.

Emmanuel began praying over a man who sort of fainted. As he fell, someone caught him and gently laid him on the floor. I was shocked. Nick and I looked at each other, wondering what had just happened.

Knowing we had questions about this unusual event, Emmanuel addressed the issue of being "slain in the Spirit." He said God's power sometimes short-circuits our bodies to allow His Holy Spirit to move through us and heal our physical and spiritual wounds. I wasn't sure if this was biblical, but I could see that it was real. The man on the floor came to and began crying and praising God as he experienced relief from past emotional wounds.

I was filled with awe and apprehension; I wondered if this African man would call me up to pray. I wanted to go up, but I was afraid. I knew I would just stand there while Emmanuel prayed and nothing special would happen. Right after I had these thoughts, his steady finger pointed my way, and up I went to get prayed for.

Nothing I had read in God's Word prepared me for what was about to happen. The Bible is full of stories recounting God touching men with His Spirit, but they seem so far removed from today that they are hard to imagine. Being skeptical, I wasn't prepared for the possibility that God might touch me that night. Was I ever in for a special surprise!

I felt like a little child as I stood there waiting for him to start praying for me. He stood a good five inches taller than I did, and his steady eyes seemed not to blink as he examined me eye to eye. I lost my courage and began looking down at my feet. I wished he would say something. It took only about thirty seconds, but it seemed like an eternity before he began to speak.

"Young man, you thought that you came home to visit your parents, but God brought you here for a divine appointment," he said. I was shocked—how did he know I was visiting my parents? "God wants to use you, but you need to forgive yourself for being weak, and you need to forgive your father for the things he has done to wound you." How did he know that about my dad?

"Lift your hands up like this," he said, showing me what to do. "I'm going to anoint your hands in the name of Jesus Christ and ask Him to heal you."

With that I lifted up my hands. He put oil on both of my hands and began to pray. Immediately I felt a burst of power coming through my hands, pulsing like an invisible ray that I could feel in my physical body. It moved through my hands about every second or two and felt like blood pulsing through my veins. This was not a physical phenomenon but a spiritual power unlike anything I have ever felt. I started to look up, but before my eyes could reach his, this power moved down my arms and legs—and then down I went.

I don't know how long I lay on that floor. It was five minutes at least, and the whole time this pulsating power was moving through my body. I was weeping and shaking and didn't care that sixty people were watching me as I lay there, unable to get up. Emmanuel started praying for Nick, and sure enough down he went. Just as I got up, Emmanuel grabbed me again and started praying powerful words that cut to the center of my heart. Down I went again, and this time I was down for the count. I felt God move through my being with healing power. This was not scary; it was gentle, loving, and very powerful.

That night Emmanuel prayed for me three separate times. Each time he prayed, I went down under God's divine power. I logged quite a bit of time on the floor that night as God began the process of changing my heart. This process is still taking place today. The Bible puts it this way: "But we all, with open face beholding as in a glass the glory of the Lord, are changed into the same image from glory to glory, even as by the Spirit of the Lord" (2 Corinthians 3:18).

Driving back to Spokane I was filled with awe. I reflected on what happened at Tillie's and wondered where this was leading. I knew God had started something special in me that night. There was no question that I looked at the world in a different way. I wanted to tell the whole world about Jesus.

Returning to work on Monday was a letdown from the weekend. I struggled to focus on my job, but something was happening inside my heart. I was losing my desire to strive for the things that worldly men hold so dear. Even my goals seemed foolish. I used to think I wanted a salary of $30,000, a new home, a nice car, and a pretty wife. That was my idea of a life. Now I just wanted to clean myself up and go to heaven with the saints of God. I longed to be in the presence of God as I had been over the weekend. If heaven is a place where you are always in God's presence, it is surely worth dying for. And if it's worth dying for, then it's also worth living for.

Shortly after the meeting at Tillie's, God visited me as I was reading His Word, and He also granted me another dream. This time I was going to know exactly what was happening in the dream and why. It was also going to give me a living picture of the Holy Spirit working through me for the purpose of preaching the gospel.

I had gone to bed early one night and I was reading the book of Job, when suddenly the words came alive. As I read the following scripture, the words became illuminated, and it felt as if God was speaking these words to me instead of me reading them: "Hast thou given the horse strength? Hast thou clothed his neck with thunder? Canst thou make him afraid as a grasshopper? The glory of his nostrils is terrible. He paweth in the valley, and rejoiceth in his strength: he goeth on to meet the armed men. He mocketh at fear, and is not affrighted; neither turneth he back from the sword. The quiver rattleth against him, the glittering spear and the shield. He swalloweth the ground with fierceness and rage. As oft as the trumpet soundeth he saith, Aha. And he smelleth the battle afar off, The thunder of the captains, and the shouting" (Job 39:19-25).

I could feel the mighty spirit that God had put inside horses of war, who willingly carried men into battle. God put that willingness inside them, and God created these magnificent animals to serve men. After that, I had the revelation and understood that the Bible was not just words. These were the true, living words of God. From that point on, I had a heavenly fear and respect for the Bible.

I lay there for quite some time thinking about why God made me. I slowly drifted to sleep to find myself in what seemed to be a look into the future. I was standing on a hill about forty feet high. It was covered with an unfamiliar type of grass, and I realized I was not in America.

A strong wind was blowing, and it seemed to be filled with God's Spirit. According to *Strong's Concordance*, the name of the Holy Spirit contains the words "wind" and "breath" in its definition. I was in what my Christian friends would call "the final hour." The power of God was moving through me, and I felt a superhuman boldness in my spirit. I was holding a wooden cross with both hands outstretched.

I looked down and saw a small band of about forty people standing at the bottom of the hill. They were all looking up at me, and I realized they were roaming around looking for food and shelter and that they were homeless because of the destruction caused by a war.

Then, as if by the command of God, I started yelling at the crowd. The words were flowing out of me like a mighty river that could not be stopped. It felt as if God's Spirit was carrying me along, and the words kept coming without the slightest effort. I knew it was God speaking through me, and I knew God was pleading with the people to repent and be saved. I also knew that not all would receive the message. With that, I bolted out of the vision.

I lay there for some time thinking about this. I felt sure it was a look into part of what God had in store for the future.

For the first time I experienced the Holy Spirit using me as a vessel for preaching the gospel. I knew that without God's Spirit, that kind of boldness was not humanly possible. Later, I found these scriptures: "But ye shall receive power, when the Holy Spirit is come upon you: and ye shall be my witnesses both in Jerusalem, and in all Judaea and Samaria, and unto the uttermost part of the earth" (Acts 1:8). And the second: "Ye are the light of the world. A city set on a hill cannot be hid. Neither do men light a lamp, and put it under the bushel, but on the stand; and it shineth unto all that are in the house" (Matthew 5:14-15).

I would not have understood the second scripture if I hadn't had this vision. When I read this passage for the first time, God's revelation power came on me, and I understood that the vision and this scripture were one and the same thing. Later I found out that this phenomenon is known as a *rhema* word from the Lord. This is where God's Spirit illuminates a passage in the Bible so that the reader understands the true meaning behind the words, for that particular moment or circumstance.

After having that vision, I understood how God's Holy Spirit worked in our lives. I was still a baby Christian, but God was beginning to move in my life. In church I learned that the God we serve is a triune God; He is three in One. "Therefore go and make disciples of all nations, baptizing them in the name of the Father, the Son and the Holy Spirit" (Matthew 28:19) — all separate and yet the same.

Jesus told His disciples that He and God were the same. This is how He put it: "Have I been so long time with you, and yet hast thou not known me, Philip? He that hath seen Me hath seen the Father; and how sayest thou then, Show us the Father?" (John 14:9). He also stated that unless He (Jesus) went away, the Comforter (Holy Spirit) would not come. This scripture says it best: "Nevertheless I tell you the truth: It is expedient for you that I go away; for if I go not away, the Comforter will not come unto you; but if I go, I will send him unto you. And he, when he is come, will convict the world in respect of sin, and of righteousness, and of judgment" (John 16:7-8).

God's Holy Spirit has been given to men to teach them, to comfort them, to instruct them, and to endue them with power. The Bible says, "And behold, I send forth the promise of My Father upon you: but tarry ye in the city, until ye be clothed with power from on high" (Luke 24:49).

What I didn't know at that time is that a person can receive a baptism in the Holy Spirit. These infillings are not a once-for-all experience; they happen repeatedly at various times when God decides to use you for His purposes. They also give a person the power to perform signs, wonders, and miracles. Remember the former scripture, "But ye shall receive power, when the Holy Spirit is come upon you" (Acts 1:8). He also gives us the power to live above the desires of sinful flesh and to live holy lives before God. "But I say, walk by the Spirit, and ye shall not fulfill the lust of the flesh" (Galatians 5:16).

Some churches do not preach this, because their pastors feel the age of miracles passed away with the death of the last apostle. Others have not yet experienced these things, and so they give little attention to the subject. Still others, however, do not believe in the true power of God, and they lead many astray with their hopeless doctrines, devoid of the truth. They do not believe God's testimony of His Son and His Holy Spirit.

The Bible has strong words for these men. It states: "This know also, that in the last days perilous times shall come. For men shall be lovers of their own selves, covetous, boasters, proud, blasphemers, disobedient to parents, unthankful, unholy, without natural affection, trucebreakers, false accusers, without self-control, fierce, despisers of those that are good, traitors, heady, high-minded, lovers of pleasures more than lovers of God; having a form of godliness, but denying the power thereof: from such turn away" (2 Timothy 3:1-5).

At the time these things were happening I was unaware of these scriptures, but God was at work in my life anyway and was about to set my life on fire with the power of His

Holy Spirit. If you have been led to believe that God's power was for the past, keep reading. Remember, the Bible clearly states: "Jesus Christ the same yesterday, and to day, and for ever" (Hebrews 13:8). He is the God of miracles, and yes, He is still at work doing miraculous things to this very day.

It was now June of 1989, and I had lived in Spokane for two years. My job had become a constant source of stress, as new management put major pressure on the field force to increase our product's share in the marketplace. Tired of living under all the pressure, I decided to take a much-needed vacation. This, I thought, would get me out of my rut and give me a chance to spend some time with my family back in Tacoma. So, I tied up the loose ends at work, and off I went, heading west for some rest and relaxation.

Visiting with my family was nice, and I felt the pressure lift as I enjoyed thinking of anything but my stressful job. I had nine days to rest and only a small list of things that I had to do. One of them was to see my good friend Nick. I couldn't wait to tell him about the mighty things that God was doing in my life. So Monday morning I was off and away to Sears to spend the morning shopping and then have lunch at our favorite place to eat, the doughnut shop.

During lunch we had a great time of reflecting and fellowship. We both poured our hearts out with great joy over the things God was doing in our lives. As we shared, we were both filled with anticipation as we wondered what God might have in store for us next. Lunch went all too quickly, and before I knew it, I was heading to mom's place with the joy of the Lord as my companion.

That night I got a call from Nick. He excitedly told me God had shown him something that He was going to do in my life. He had called to see if I could go to church with him on Sunday because God was going to meet me there for a special purpose. I gladly accepted this invitation and I anticipated what God might do. The rest of the week flew by, and before I knew it we were standing in the midst of the congregation praising our Lord and Savior Jesus Christ.

Things seemed fairly normal, and I was beginning to think that Nick might have missed God on this one. Then the pastor began preaching on the power of God, the Holy Spirit. And just as Emmanuel had preached, he began giving some of the same convincing scriptures to prove that God wanted to pour out His Spirit on all the believers of Christ. He read about the gifts of the Spirit: "For to one is given through the Spirit the word of wisdom; and to another the word of knowledge, according to the same Spirit: to another faith, in the same Spirit; and to another gifts of healings, in the one Spirit; and to another workings of miracles; and to another prophecy; and to another discernings of spirits; to another divers kinds of tongues; and to another the interpretation of tongues: but all these worketh the one and the same Spirit, dividing to each one severally even as he will" (1 Corinthians 12:8-11).

After hearing the list of gifts, I decided I wanted them all. What I didn't count on is that God was going to give me some of them that very day. As I sat thinking about God's awesome power, the pastor began asking all who would like to receive the Holy Spirit to raise their hands. Without thinking, my right hand instantly shot up, as if it had a mind of its own. Being shy by nature, I meant to put my hand down, but instead it kept going even higher. The pastor then asked all who raised their hands to come up front.

As I walked forward my heart started racing, and I asked myself what I was doing in this church in the first place. We lined up in front of the pulpit, and then a group of elders and helpers escorted us to a room behind the main sanctuary. I'll never forget the young man assigned to pray with me. I was 32 at the time, and I guessed him to be no older than 25. This was a blessing, because I was somewhat intimidated by the men in the church, so God arranged for a young man to pray with me so I would feel safe.

As we sat down to talk I noticed he was a bit nervous. He seemed out of his comfort zone, and I wanted to ask him if this was his first time praying for someone. Instead, I fell back on my sales experience and took control of the conversation. This always makes people feel relaxed, because I can make statements or ask questions, and they don't have to work so hard at making small talk. I began by telling him about the things God had done in my life. He was fascinated and began to relax. This was great, because we both loved the Lord, and now we had common ground so we could read God's Word and pray together.

For about ten minutes he told me about the Holy Spirit and read many scriptures explaining the relationship we have with the Comforter. Then he read this scripture: "And they of the circumcision that believed were amazed, as many as came with Peter, because that on the Gentiles also was poured out the gift of the Holy Spirit. For they heard them speak with tongues, and magnify God" (Acts 10:45-46).

After reading that scripture, he asked if I would like to receive the Holy Spirit and have the evidence of speaking in tongues. That was the very thing I came to receive, so naturally I said yes. He then asked me to join him in a simple prayer: "Almighty Father, Your Word says that if we receive Jesus as Lord and Savior, we can also receive the baptism of the Holy Spirit. Lord, we have received Your Son, Jesus, and now ask that you fill us with Your Holy Spirit according to the promise in Your Word. It is written that 'everyone who asks receives and everyone who seeks finds. "Lord, we now receive Your Spirit by faith. Amen."

He told me to open my mouth and let the Spirit of God take over. I did open my mouth, and something supernatural did happen. All of a sudden my mouth and tongue sped up faster than my mind could go. Out of my mouth came this language that had a heavenly origin. This was unlike any language I had ever heard. In fact, it was much faster than any language on earth. By that I mean that my tongue was moving at many times its normal speed.

Even my ears had to fight to catch up, and it felt as if my mouth and tongue were disconnected from my mind and were connected to God. This startled the young man who had prayed with me. He jumped out of his seat and started yelling, "He has it! He has it!" He called to the other men to come and see for themselves. He was as shocked as I was about this miracle.

It was over in a short time, and then a feeling of wonder came over me. This experience was so powerful and supernatural I could hardly process the feelings moving through me. God had just spoken out of my mouth. This turned out to be a life-changing event for me. I couldn't wait to tell Nick. I hurried out of the back room after hugging that guy and thanking him for praying with me.

Nick was beaming with joy; he already knew what had happened. He then confessed that God had shown him in a vision that He was going to baptize me in the Holy Spirit and showed him Sthe church He was going to do this in. We spent the rest of the day praising God and reading our Bibles at our favorite restaurant.

Speaking in tongues is a delicate subject that has separated well-meaning believers and caused division in the church. I found this was also the case back in the days of the early church. The true believers had received this gift along with the baptism of the Holy Spirit. But other people did not recognize this as a move of God. They criticized the gift by accusing believers of being drunk:

And when the day of Pentecost was fully come, they were all with one accord in one place. And suddenly there came a sound from heaven as of a rushing mighty wind, and it filled all the house where they were sitting. And there appeared unto them cloven tongues like as of fire, and it sat upon each of them. And they were all filled with the Holy Ghost, and began to speak with other tongues, as the Spirit gave them utterance. Now there were dwelling at Jerusalem Jews, devout men, from every nation under heaven. And when this sound was heard, the multitude came together, and were confounded, because that every man heard them speaking in his own language. And they were all amazed and marvelled, saying, "Behold, are not all these that speak Galilaeans? And how hear we, every man in our own language wherein we were born? Parthians and Medes and Elamites, and the dwellers in Mesopotamia, in Judaea and Cappadocia, in Pontus and Asia, in Phrygia and Pamphylia, in Egypt and the parts of Libya about Cyrene, and sojourners from Rome, both Jews and proselytes, Cretans and Arabians, we hear them speaking in our tongues the mighty works of God." And they were all amazed, and were perplexed, saying one to another, "What meaneth this?" But others, mocking, said, "They are filled with new wine!" (Acts 2:13).

There is another type of tongues that no one can understand. This is the type I spoke at church. The Bible calls it the "tongues of angels," and this type of tongues can only be understood by the gift of interpretation given by the Holy Spirit: "If any man speaketh in a tongue, let it be by two, or at the most three, and that in turn; and let one interpret: but if there be no interpreter, let him keep silence in the church; and let him speak to himself, and to God" (1 Corinthians 14:28).

The main purpose of this type of tongues is that in times of need, when we do not know what to pray or how to pray, we can let the Holy Spirit take over by praying in the Spirit: "Likewise the Spirit also helpeth our infirmities: for we know not what we should pray for as we ought: but the Spirit itself maketh intercession for us with groanings which cannot be uttered" (Romans 8:26). This allows the Holy Spirit to take over and pray the exact, perfect prayer needed for each situation. This gift is a powerful weapon in the warfare against the devil and his demons.

As I headed back to Spokane this time, I went with the feeling that I was somehow a different man. Something had happened to me that changed my thinking about God and His role in my life. I knew that the course of my life had been altered. God had given me His Spirit for a reason. He was now leading me in a new direction and, with all the faith that God had given me, I was going to follow. I didn't know the final destination or the path I was to walk, but I didn't care, because God leading me, and I knew I was going to find my promised land.

♦ 6 ♦

The Devil and
His Demons—For Real

Receiving the baptism of the Holy Spirit was a turning
point in my walk with God. With the power of God
working in my life, things were going to change in my
Christian walk. The Holy Spirit has a way of motivating
a person to minister the gospel every chance he gets. The
one thing I didn't count on, however, was that I now had an
enemy to contend with, and he wasn't going to sit back and
let me preach everyone into the kingdom of God.

I was going to find out the hard way that the devil is real,
and his demons actively fight the saints of God. We need not
be afraid, however. The Bible declares: "Ye are of God, my
little children, and have overcome them: because greater is
He that is in you than he that is in the world" (l John 4:4).

The fact that I'm still serving the Lord with increasing
devotion is living proof of this. Not all Christians go through
the kind of attacks I'm going to tell about. In fact, I have
met only a handful of Christians that have had experiences
like mine. I just figured Satan had tried to stop my Christian
testimony before it had a chance to take root and produce
good fruit for the Lord.

These events started even before I knew the Lord and have continued in lesser frequency to this day. Right after I started going to church, the enemy started intruding into my life. It was springtime, and I had just received Jesus as Lord and Savior. I remember thinking that nothing could be nicer than to be a Christian and have a whole lifetime to live for the Lord. The last thing on my mind was demons, devils, and evil thoughts. That is why I was so shocked when, out of nowhere, I was severely attacked by Satan and his demons.

One Sunday afternoon after a great church service, I was talking about the Lord with a friend. I was interrupted by the most disgusting voice I have ever heard. I heard this voice shout in my right ear, "Hurt her!" I stopped talking, and my arms and legs went numb with fear. This was no joke, and it wasn't my imagination. Not knowing what to do, I pretended I had a headache to avoid confessing what had just happened.

The rest of the day I walked around in a daze. My nerves were shot, and I went pale from fear. I had just received the Lord and had not yet heard about demons that actually attack people using bad thoughts or evil voices. Not knowing this left me feeling confused and scared, so I tried to put it out of my mind and went about the rest of my day.

That night I was to have dinner with my folks. I was looking forward to this and hoped I would feel better after spending time with people I trust. The night started out pretty normal. We all sat around making small talk as my mom cooked. Dinner was just about ready.

As my mom began to set the table, I felt the enemy attack me physically, leaving me in a state of pure horror. That night we were having steak, so my mom pulled out the steak knives to put them by our plates. When I saw the knives, the most horrible sharp pain pierced my stomach, sending an intense burning sensation through my entire body. I doubled over and groaned as the agony of this attack went through my body. It actually felt as if a sharp knife had stabbed me. My parents stared as I bent over in pain. When they asked me what was wrong, I lied and told them I had a stomachache. I sat there for what seemed to be an eternity as I tried to regain my composure and act as if nothing was wrong.

Dinner was a nightmare. What was happening to me? Why was the devil attacking me? I ate what I could of my meal and then excused myself and went home. I never said a word to my folks about the day's events, and my silence was killing me. I needed someone to tell me that I was all right. I felt as if I was losing my mind. The fear had been so gripping that I could hardly swallow my food at dinner.

I got into bed that night and wondered what all this meant. As I lay there I noticed something filling my room—an evil presence. Before I had a chance to get out of bed, this thing started smothering me from head to foot. It was the devil himself, and he was choking me. I began to gasp for air, and my body started to twist to the side as if I was deformed or crippled. I watched my hands begin to contort in a way that was totally evil; my legs were tucked up behind my back as if I was a paraplegic.

Then, with my eyes wide open, I saw ripping flesh. I could feel the total hatred that it takes to murder a person. I was on the brink of vomiting. Suddenly I yelled, "God, help me!" Instantly it all went away, leaving me in a pile of broken pieces that I thought could never be put back in order.

I had just tasted hell itself. I knew how a killer feels when he murders someone. This thing surrounded me, and I could feel the hate and the murderous thoughts that Satan has toward human beings. It was so horrible that just thinking about it is difficult.

This started a wave of attacks that lasted three solid years. Every night I would go to bed wondering when this evil presence would show up to harass me. I became so fearful at times that I thought I was going to lose my mind. I would walk around stiff and as white as a ghost. My family began to ask me about all this, and I had no answers.

During this time I learned how to lean on the Lord. I found that the name of Jesus, when used in faith, was more than enough to settle the score with the enemy. It took three years of prayers and crying out before this thing finally left me for good. After that I was free from the life-threatening fear that had gripped me to the point of death.

Unfortunately for me, the church I attended never taught about demon attacks and didn't teach us how to engage in spiritual warfare. I had been a sitting duck for the enemy. I had no idea how to fight the devil and his demons. It was a painful learning process. I often asked God why He allowed this to come into my life, but all I got in return was the scripture that says: "My grace is sufficient for thee!"

After my three-year battle with Satan was over, I came out a new man. I was more solid and steadfast and much more serious about the things of the Spirit. Through all these battles I have developed a healthy respect for the blood of Jesus and its power over the enemy. The Bible says, "They overcame him by the blood of the Lamb, and by the word of their testimony; and they loved not their lives unto the death" (Revelation 12:11).

Without the precious blood of Jesus I am convinced that I would not be here today. Since those days I have had many encounters with the enemy, and each encounter convinces me even more that we have the victory in Christ Jesus. Many of my encounters with Satan came in the night visions and I am going to share a couple of these events so you will get the idea.

In a dream I watched Satan coming out of a desolate wilderness and walking straight towards me. He was coming out of a barren desert. All I could see was sand and dead trees.

Satan looked like a normal man in his 60s. I had revelation knowledge in this dream, so I knew this was no ordinary man. This was the enemy of Christ—the devil, Satan. He walked up and stood facing me about five feet away. We were staring eye to eye as if sizing each other up. I wondered why he had come to speak with me.

After sizing me up, he pointed his right finger in my face and said, "I'm going to destroy your family." Not even moved a bit by his threats, I responded, "Satan, you cannot touch my family; they are covered in the blood of Jesus!" Satan stood motionless with his eyes to the ground, as if in deep thought. Then he lifted up his head and responded, "But I can give you AIDS." I pointed back in his face and said, "You might be able to give me AIDS, but all that will mean to me is that I will go home early to be with my Father who is in heaven. So in Jesus' name, depart!"

As I said these words, I was pointing my right finger in the direction of the barren desert as if to say, "Go back home where you belong!" It took about three seconds of staring at each other before he turned and headed back to where he came from. I kept my finger pointing the whole time, and after about ten steps he turned back to see if I meant what I had said. Seeing that I was unmovable, he turned again and went off into the distance.

This encounter gave me great hope. For one thing, I came away with a new understanding of the authority we have in Jesus Christ. None of my family members were born again at the time I had this encounter; when I woke from this dream I realized that God had been protecting my family, even though they had not yet received Jesus as Lord and Savior. I thanked God for His divine protection and started to pray for my family to receive Jesus as soon as possible.

A year later I had another encounter with Satan that taught me something about God's love and the way He sees His children. In a dream I was standing in front of a huge brick wall. It was so large I cannot remember seeing the sides and could not see the top. A mist floated down from above and formed the face of Jesus. It was illuminated, and I remember thinking that it looked like a hologram.

Suddenly, out of the center of this hologram, Satan came rushing directly at me. He pointed his right finger at me and shook it in total anger. He was furious. His face was red, and his eyes burned with hate toward me. As he came closer, he began shouting, "You think you are a man of God; you can't be a man of God! You drink Old Granddad whiskey!" At the time I was still drinking to relieve the stress, and Old Granddad was my favorite brand of whiskey.

The Bible calls Satan the great accuser of the saints of God, and in this vision he was out to accuse me. In an instant I experienced the guilt of knowing that my drinking was not pleasing to God, but I also knew that someday I was going to get victory over this habit.

All of a sudden the Holy Spirit came upon me in a powerful way, filling me with authority. I pointed my finger at Satan and rebuked him with these words: "Satan, God's kingdom is not of eating or drinking!" These words, spoken with the power of the Holy Spirit, stopped Satan in his tracks, turned him around, and sent him heading in the other direction.

I then noticed a door to my left. I went through it and found myself face-to-face with Satan one more time. He began accusing me of all sorts of things. I cannot remember what scripture I spoke, but it ended the encounter instantly and for good.

Waking from this dream, I was full of thanksgiving. Even though I was still drinking, God loved me and allowed me to put Satan to flight with the Word of God and the power of the Holy Spirit. I was determined to get clean before God and serve Him with all that was within me. A few years later, I came upon this scripture: "For the kingdom of God is not eating and drinking, but righteousness and peace and joy in the Holy Spirit" (Romans 14:17).

In another dream I received a vivid picture of the protection God provides for His children. This dream started with me waking from another dream. I awoke in this dream to see hundreds of little black handkerchiefs all around my bed. It looked as if they were being kept at a distance by some unseen force. I watched as these black patches moved in an erratic motion, looking for a chance to get inside the boundary that held them back. They were everywhere, and they had slits for eyes and claw-like fingers that ended in razor-sharp fingernails. These were demons trying to attack me while I slept.

Suddenly the scene changed. In an instant I was out of my body, viewing this event from a different viewpoint. As I examined the scene, I could see what was keeping the demons from destroying me: an invisible shield was over my bed. The demons were frantically looking for a way in, but this shield was perfect, and their efforts were futile. I then relaxed, and with the shield of the Lord as my cover, I fell back asleep with peace in my heart.

Months later I came across a scripture that reminded me not to be afraid of the terror by night: "...who are kept guarded (shielded) by the power of God through faith for salvation ready to be revealed in the last time" (1 Peter 1:5). God is going to guard all those who put their trust in Him through the power of His Holy Spirit until the day of Christ, when Jesus comes to claim us for His own.

The devil and his demons are real. I have seen them and dealt with them. I have told about only a few of my encounters, as God has led me. But these things are real and very dangerous to fool with.

The only safety a person can find against these powers is the blood of Jesus and the power of the Holy Spirit. In today's world people dabble in dangerous areas by calling on demon powers through false religions, the occult, and New Age practices. People are seduced by demon spirits through the desire to know the future and the lust to gain spiritual powers through channeling and witchcraft.

The Bible is very clear on this subject. It offers grave warnings to people who follow after these things. In the end, all that go this way will end up in the lake of fire where Satan and his followers will be tormented day and night, forever and ever. If you have been caught in one of Satan's traps, it is not too late. The Bible says that if a sinner turns back from his evil ways and repents, God will forgive him, save him, and cleanse him of all unrighteousness.

◆ 7 ◆

Miracles in Motion

~~~

S hortly after I received the baptism of the Holy Spirit, the
Lord made a way for me to move back to my hometown
of Tacoma. This was by God's leading, because just after
moving back, I began moving in the new gifts that God had
given me. I also began an in-depth study of God's Word. I
began attending Christian meetings as often as possible and
visited as many Bible studies as my busy schedule allowed.
This was a turning point in my Christian walk, because it
was there that I started moving in my gifts. God's Holy Spirit
began to use me as a vessel for His glory.

Before the miracles in the meetings started, He confirmed
His call on my life in two wonderful dreams. In the first
dream, I was standing before my paternal grandmother. She
was lying in the center of a huge bed, bigger than any king-
sized bed I had ever seen. I knew she was bedridden because
of an accident, but I didn't know the nature of the accident.
As I looked on, I began to ask myself why I was being shown
this. It startled me, because even though I loved my grandmother, I seldom got to see her.

As I stood there wondering about this unusual sight, two
identical blond-haired women suddenly appeared out of thin
air. They were standing on the two end corners of the bed

looking down on me, and it startled me to see them standing at military-like attention. They were alike in every way, down to the color and style of their hair. Both were wearing nurse's uniforms, and I got the impression these uniforms represented something supernatural. They were motionless like statues, not moving or breathing, and I wondered what this could mean. Then the woman on my right suddenly came to life. Instantly, I knew by revelation that the woman on my left represented the world and the one on my right represented God's kingdom in heaven.

As she became animated, she looked down at me and said, "God has sent me here to prophesy to you." Having said that, she stepped down off the bed and walked right up to me. She looked into my eyes and said, "Give me your right hand." She reached down and gently took hold of my hand.

With my right hand in hers she said, "The Lord God has called you to preach the gospel of Jesus Christ to thousands and thousands of people who are dying and going to hell because they do not know Jesus. He has chosen you to help deliver this message to the people. God has also chosen you to reign in heaven with Him forever and ever."

After she spoke that last set of words, I instantly knew God had a special office or position for me in heaven. I was stunned to think of myself having an important position in heaven, because on earth I have been what most people would consider a very common man. By that I mean I was unemployed a lot of the time, was sick with many ailments, and lacked self-esteem.

As I pondered these wonderful words from God, my mind was opened up by the power of the Holy Spirit. Instantly the knowledge of what it's like to be in heaven was poured into my being. This revelation hit me like a speeding bullet, and down I went to the ground as if I had been hit by a ton of bricks. I could taste heaven, and it was wonderful beyond description. It was so wonderful that a small taste was enough to knock me to the ground.

I hit the ground and was weeping and moaning and crying in an inhuman way. These tears were tears not of mourning but of joy unspeakable and relief—relief because I realized I was going to make it. I felt total relief knowing how undeserving of heaven I was and understanding that I was going there anyway.

I was going to heaven because Jesus secured my place two thousand years ago on the cross. I was to enter a place so wonderful that human lips cannot begin to describe it. This heavenly encounter ended with me lying on the ground sobbing and the woman from heaven still holding my right hand. With that, I came out of this dream to find my pillow wet with tears and my heart still warmed by this most unusual event.

As I lay there, this scripture came into my mind: "For many are called, but few are chosen" (Matthew 22:14). I was filled with awe knowing that God had chosen me to serve Him in the ministry, and this dream confirmed it. This has been and still is my heart's desire.

A week later, my grandmother fell and broke her hip. She was laid up for quite a while. I knew God had shown me this ahead of time to confirm that it was a true message from heaven.

Two weeks later I had yet another dream that confirmed God had decided to use me. Jesus said to His disciples, "Come ye after Me, and I will make you fishers of men" (Matthew 4:19). In this second dream, I was standing on a hill overlooking the most beautiful river I had ever seen. Its color reminded me of the crystal pond mentioned earlier; it was gently moving along at a slow pace. On both sides of the riverbank men were holding fishing poles and casting their lines into the water. As I watched, not one fish was caught.

Then a man walked up to me holding the most unusual fishing pole that I had ever seen. This pole was about five feet long and was at least four inches around from bottom to top. It looked more like a five-foot club than a fishing pole. He handed it to me, and I looked at it in wonder. I had never seen such a sight and didn't know what to think about this unusual event. Seeing my confusion, the man exclaimed: "Scott, you are going to be catching big fish." I was then shown a huge white box. I knew the day's catch was inside and wondered how we had done. The man opened the box. It was full to the brim with beautiful large salmon.

After seeing this wonderful sight, I woke up and thanked God for His blessing. I knew what He meant about catching big fish. He was telling me I was going to catch men for God. I also got the feeling that some of them were going to be "big fish" or influential people. I remember thinking about writing a book about the miraculous dreams and miracles I had seen. That idea kept rolling over in my mind, but who was I to think that I could write a book?

At the same time, Nick started having dreams from the Lord. They mainly focused on his personal walk with Jesus, but some were awesome pictures of coming events. Something started happening to both of us about this time. Every time we would meet to discuss God, this beautiful feeling would come over us, and we would get goose bumps from head to toe.

These goose bumps came every time we mentioned the name of Jesus and would be quite powerful at times. Since then I have come to know this phenomenon as the anointing of God. This is the terminology for God's power resting on a person. To this day I get goose bumps whenever I discuss the glory of God and His Son, Jesus. At times, when the anointing is strong, my eyes will shut. I've had many visions sitting with my eyes closed and my arms full of those little bumps.

One night Nick and I went over to Tillie's house to see a video of a television evangelist. We had never heard of him, and Tillie was excited to have us watch him preach and pray for people during one of his TV crusades. As we sat on the couch talking, I started to feel this power building in the room. It was building slowly, and I knew God was about to do something supernatural.

At that point Tillie loaded the tape in the player, and we settled down to watch the video. The program began with a special prayer to open the meeting. All of a sudden I heard a loud voice in my right ear. I knew this was the voice of God. I heard the Lord saying, "Jesus, cleanse me with Your blood." Before I could react, I immediately heard the man on the tape pray, "Jesus, cleanse me with Your blood."

A wave of God's power swept across the couch and almost knocked us over. It moved through Nick, and when it hit me it felt like hot oil moving through my body. I am pretty sure it was the blood of Jesus moving through me. Tillie watched from the lounge chair as God moved through us, and we spent the rest of the night praising God for His presence and reading His Word.

With the last event fresh in our minds, we started to wonder why the Lord would spend so much energy on men like us. I guess I felt He was doing similar things with all His children. I wished the whole world could have felt that heavenly cleansing, and yet the people I shared this story with seemed unmoved by my testimony. They either didn't believe the testimony, or they just didn't care. Either way, my heart broke each time I would testify to the great things that God had done, only to have my words fall on deaf ears. Why people reject the works of God remains a mystery to me.

Shortly after this I quit my job with the publishing company. This was great for stress reduction, but it didn't pay the bills too well, so I began looking for a new career.

One day while looking in the employment section of the local newspaper, the Lord gave me the idea to design and market Christian T-shirts. My ex-boss and good friend Bill Dahlgren had been forced into early retirement and needed something to do, so we became business partners in this venture.

We didn't do much in the way of business, but for six months the Lord had me commuting from Tacoma to Beaverton, Oregon, as we developed new T-shirt designs and tried to find a market for them. Little did I realize that God had other plans for bringing me to Beaverton, and they had nothing to do with T-shirts. He showed me in a vision that I was to go in another direction. It was difficult to tell Bill what the Lord had shown me. We both resisted the message God had given me in the following dream but nevertheless prayed for the Lord's will.

In this dream, I found myself on an animated pathway. I say animated because it looked almost like a cartoon. The path was perfectly straight. As I looked ahead I could see the path split in two directions. As I came to the Y in the path, I stopped. I wasn't sure which way to go and Suddenly, I could see in both directions at the same time, as if my eyes were independent of each other. As I looked to the left I saw a strange sight. Floating up in the air I could see our T-shirt designs slowly spinning in different directions. The designs were as large as a house, and the overall picture looked like a huge mobile in motion.

I immediately said, "This is the way we are to go," and without looking to the right I headed off to the left. I took exactly three steps when I heard the voice of the Lord behind me say: "My son, you have to go in the other direction." Hearing this, I backed up and followed the path to the right.

When I awoke from this dream, I knew God wanted me to go in a different direction. He had a different path for me to follow, and it headed in a new direction that I could not see. I picked up the phone to give Bill the bad news.

He was less than pleased with this information, because he had invested a lot of time and money in this project. Both of us wanted to do God's will, so we prayed for guidance and left the rest up to the Lord. Not long after this, it became apparent that God was not blessing our business. After much prayer and meditation, we finally humbled ourselves to the will of the Lord and chose new directions.

About a month later, I came across this scripture: "And thine ears shall hear a word behind thee, saying, this is the way, walk ye in it, when ye turn to the right hand, and when ye turn to the left" (Isaiah 30:21).

So now I needed a real job. Bill and I said goodbye to our business plans and made a commitment to remain good friends. Shortly after this, my friend Steve Johnson called and offered me another job with the company he was currently working for. He had been my job finder most of my adult life and my answer to him was "Yes, I do!" Without any effort, I secured a great-paying job, in the nick of time. I have come to find out that God works this way. Just when all seems lost, here comes the Lord with the answer to your problem. Praise be unto our God forever and ever. Amen.

So there I was returning to sales, even though I was not meant for that kind of work. The sad thing is that I was slipping deeper and deeper into depression and did not realize it. My new job was very stressful. I wanted nothing to do with sales, but I was stuck. All I wanted was to serve God. I kept reminding the Lord of His promise to use me. With a ton of financial pressure on my shoulders, I turned my attention to my new job and struggled to keep a positive attitude.

This left me feeling lost and confused. Why was I having so much pain in my life if God was on my side? I began having panic attacks, which left me feeling dead inside and my doctor put me on antidepressants. I felt as if God had turned His back on me.

I was learning the hard lesson that being used by God can entail pressure and sorrow and pain. The closer I got to Jesus, the harder my life seemed to be. Not knowing the principle of godly suffering, I was losing hope that God was still on my side. Little did I know that God was about to pour out His Spirit on my life and give me the hope I desperately needed.

I remained in communication with my former business partner Bill. That was great for me, because Bill was like a father figure to me. He was kind and gave me advice that I could count on. One night Bill called to tell me about this great Bible study meeting he had found. He was excited about the things God had been doing and wondered if I would come to the next meeting.

Needing a touch from God, I accepted his invitation and went the following weekend in hopes that God would touch me at the meeting. I was unaware that God was going to meet me in a big way at this meeting, and I would come away with something I didn't even know I needed—the fear of the Lord.

Hoping to get a good seat in the meeting, Bill and I arrived early. I felt comfortable meeting the hosts, Lynn Gangle and his wife, Connie. It was apparent from the start that they loved the Lord and enjoyed having meetings in their home. So we relaxed and had a good time of fellowship before the meeting got started.

Bill had told me the meetings were usually packed, so it was disappointing when the grand total came to seven people. This was unusual, they said, as normally they would have eighteen to thirty people attend each week. I suddenly had an overwhelming feeling that God had ordered this meeting, and I was going to be the guest of honor.

One by one each person gave a short testimony about the Lord and how God had been working in their lives. I gave my testimony last, and that is when the atmosphere began to change.

I had just poured my heart out about my encounters with God when Lynn started asking me a series of questions centered on my walk with the Lord. After that, he prayed in tongues for about three minutes. We were seated across the room from him and sat patiently while he prayed.

Then he said, "Scott, the Lord is going to use you mightily in ways you cannot understand at this time. Because of this, the enemy has come against you even when you were young. Before the Lord can use you, He needs to break the spiritual cords that bind you and have come through generational curses. He wants me to pray them off right now. Is that OK?"

Back then I knew nothing about generational curses and spiritual cords that can bind a man, but I wanted nothing to do with having curses on me, so I said yes. He started praying. The words he prayed didn't sound loud or powerful, but as soon as he started to pray, something happened to me.

A powerful force came down upon me and filled my body from head to toe. I began to shake and quiver as he continued praying. I was shaking badly, and my body temperature went way up. I started to sweat like never before, completely soaking my shirt and fogging up my glasses. I started panting hard, like a woman in labor, and I became worried because this power kept on coming and I was unable to stop it. I started sobbing and was about to yell out, "Stop, stop, I can't take anymore!" when the experience ended.

Just then Lynn quit praying, and I felt a release as this power lifted off of me. I collapsed back on the couch, relieved and shocked at what had just taken place. My mind was reeling with questions, my body was weak from the power drain, and I was trembling as the room grew silent.

Thinking this is what God wanted to do for the night, I let my mind relax. Just then, as I thought things were going to let up, I suddenly felt Jesus' presence. I knew He was standing at my right side and yet I could not see him. At the exact moment that I realized this, Lynn started speaking again.

"Jesus is here, Scott, and He needs to give you something." Instantly a bolt of power like lightning came from the place where Jesus was standing. It was flowing from Jesus right into my mind through my temple. It felt as if Jesus was putting something into my mind, and He was doing it at lightning speed. The power was so intense that I groaned out loud. It was over in about five seconds, and then all was silent.

I began crying and asking out loud, "What is going on here? Jesus, what are You doing to me?" Then I felt a calm come over me. I was in the presence of the Lord, and He was comforting me with His presence.

Then Lynn spoke again. "Scott, Jesus is going to show you something, something very special." Suddenly I had my first open vision. My eyes began to see a different place, a heavenly place. I was standing on a pathway that looked animated with vivid color. The pathway went up a gentle slope and split in two directions before disappearing over the top of a small hill. As soon as my eyes focused on this path, two men robed in white whisked smoothly by. They seemed almost transparent. My eyes followed them to the top of the hill where they stopped to join others who had gathered at the Y in the path.

As I watched, a light shone down on the people in white robes, and they all looked up. My eyes followed, and I looked up also. Then I saw Jesus in the sky, with His arms outstretched as if He was still on the cross. He was actually glowing like metal when it is melted at a high temperature. The glory of God shone down on the saints, and His radiance filled my eyes with heavenly light and engulfed my soul.

I burst out crying and was overwhelmed by this open vision. My mind was reeling. I kept repeating, "Jesus, You're so beautiful, You're so beautiful." This vision lasted for two or three minutes. Then as suddenly as it had started, the vision vanished. I sat there for a few moments trying to gather my thoughts as people in the room asked me questions about what I had just seen. Could this be real? I knew I had just seen Jesus in a vision, but somehow it was just too incredible to believe. The Bible says we will see visions: "And it shall come to pass afterward, that I will pour out my spirit upon all flesh; and your sons and your daughters shall prophesy, your old men shall dream dreams, your young men shall see visions" (Joel 2:28). I guess I was getting a practical lesson on the truth of the scriptures.

I have since learned that if the Bible says we are going to see visions, then we are going to see visions. If it says we are going to dream dreams, then we can count on dreaming dreams. This is pretty simple to say but hard to believe. That is, unless you take the Word of God at face value and believe God is real. He means what He says and says what He means.

After discussing this vision in detail, we began to praise the Lord, wondering what He would do next. That is when Lynn began to prophesy about my ministry. He gave me encouraging words that confirmed what God had already spoken to me. After that, Lynn grabbed a chair and put it in the middle of the living room. It was time to anoint me with oil, he said, and ask the Lord to fill me with His power.

As I sat there waiting, I was filled with awe. This was the most incredible night. I could barely believe this was actually happening, yet here I was, still shaking from the touch of the Lord, and yes, this was real.

With the bottle of oil in his hand, Lynn began to pray. He was standing in front of me, and the words he spoke were filled with God's power. I began to shake all over just as I had earlier.

Then Lynn anointed my forehead with oil and began asking God to fill me with His Holy Spirit. Immediately after anointing me, a burst of power shot up from the center of my being. It came from way down inside my being and moved with great power up and out of my mouth. It was that heavenly language again. But this time it came out with such power that it felt as if the whole earth would be shaken by these powerful words.

Out of my mouth came this heavenly language with such power that I actually leaned forward due to the surge of energy. It felt as if God had control of my tongue, my lips, and my belly as these words roared out of me like air bursting out of a balloon. The words flowed out of me for about a minute, and I was almost yelling as they came forth with the might of a lion's roar.

Just as these powerful words ceased, I felt the Lord come straight down from above and fill me with His presence. This wasn't anything like the feeling of speaking in tongues. It actually felt as if God filled me with His presence. Before I could even think, God began speaking out of my mouth, and I knew this was the English version of what was spoken in tongues. I later found out this is called the gift of interpretation of tongues.

These are the exact words that came flowing out of me: "My words are trustworthy and true. Those that have put their trust in Me will not be ashamed. I have Satan under My right foot, and I will crush him at the appointed time. Those that have put their trust in My Son, Jesus, will have eternal life. I have spoken it in My Word, and so shall it be. Those that wait upon Me will renew their strength; they shall mount up with wings as eagles, they shall run and not be weary and they shall walk and not faint." These words were powerful, and for the second time, I felt the absolute authority that only

God has. I knew that nothing in the heavens or on the earth or under the earth could go against what was just said.

Suddenly another powerful thing happened. Just after these words came out of my mouth, the Lord gave a word of prophecy to all of us. Through my mouth, God began to give each one in the room a promise of gifts to come. Before God did this, He closed my ears so I could hear absolutely nothing. Like a puppet on a string, my right hand pointed to each person in turn as I felt my mouth pronouncing the promise. I was the last person to receive a word, and my hand actually pointed back at myself as God spoke words over my life. Why He wouldn't let me hear these prophecies remains a mystery. I asked Him in prayer and got no answer.

After this move of God, we were all gripped with a heavenly fear. God's power is real, and He is holy. I left that night with the understanding that God is to be revered. To treat Him with anything but total reverence would be foolish.

I also left with a new understanding of God and His ways. On the way out the door, Lynn gave me one more word from the Lord. He said that for three days I would be filled with God's power, and I would begin to minister the Word of God. As it turned out, he was right. For three days God moved through me, bringing powerful words to the people God wanted me to speak to.

Arriving back in Tacoma after that special night felt like touching down on earth after a successful walk on the moon. I had come back to earth only to find that I was still Scott Madsen. I still had a boss, and that boss still needed the same sales figures to increase in the same sales territory. Somehow I expected everything to be different since God had just filled me with His power not more than thirty hours earlier.

I was still in the training phase of my new job, and I was being torn between thoughts of God and His kingdom and the thoughts that dominate a person in the constant struggle to get by. But I learned that the Lord's presence can transform an ordinary workday into a day of miracles.

It was the Monday morning following that miraculous evening in Oregon. I woke with anticipation, because the power of God had been with me, just as Lynn had said. I was still in training, and I headed north to meet my new trainer, Dan. I was to meet him at his apartment to review the files and go over the territory boundaries in our sales area. As we discussed these things, I began to feel God's presence building in the room.

Dan suddenly put down his files and began telling me about his ex-wife. He confessed that she had left him without even telling him why. Knowing that I was a Christian, he wanted to ask me why God would allow this to happen, because he loved her very much and worked hard to make his marriage a good one. As he poured out his heart, I felt the Lord filling me with revelation power. Suddenly, I knew why she had left him, and I knew in detail some of the hurtful things she had done against their marriage. I was getting pretty excited at this point, because this was the first time God had shown me something I could not know in such detail. I suddenly said, "Dan, God has just shown me why your wife left. Do you want to know?"

He responded with a big yes, and I started to pour out what God had just shown me. As my words hit his ears he began to cry. He kept saying yes, yes, that is exactly right. He then admitted that she later confessed to doing exactly what God had just shown me.

Seizing the moment, I began to minister to Dan with the wisdom God had given me. It was awesome, sitting there pouring out God's comfort to a hurting soul. As I kept pouring it out, God's glory began to fill the entire apartment. Both of us felt the heavenly presence as it engulfed us. Enveloped by God's Spirit, Dan kept saying, "God's presence is all around me, all around me—I can feel it, I can feel it!"

That was quite a day. We didn't get much worldly work done, but we got quite a bit done for God's kingdom. Dan was able to feel God's presence for the first time, and this compelled him to seek the Lord with all his heart.

That night I went to bed a happy man. God had done exactly as Lynn prophesied. For three days I was filled with God's power, and for three days I ministered to people in the true power of God. This gave me a respect for prophecy and taught me not to dismiss a word simply because it seems too fantastic to be true. I learned later to test each word against the Bible to see if it lines up with God's pattern of truth, clearly laid down for us to follow. Failure to do this can land you in spiritual left field in a heartbeat.

After that night in Oregon, my walk with God took a turn in a new direction. That night set the miracles in motion, and I was to find out later that the best was yet to come.

The Word Comes Alive

Ministering to Dan became a part-time job. He trained me to present our products while I trained him in the things God had shown me. This was a very pleasant arrangement, and I have fond memories of those days.

I worked in Tacoma for the next six months and then swapped territories with the Oregon representative, hoping my life would improve with a change of address. During those days I struggled with an identity crisis. God was speaking to me—this I knew without question. I kept asking myself why I was still out in the selling field when I should be out in the harvest field preaching the gospel of Jesus Christ to a hurting and broken world. Not having the answer to this puzzling question, I felt empty and lost. I was hoping God would open a door to the ministry, but I had to learn the hard way that God only sends people out when they are ready to be sent and not one day sooner.

Waiting on the Lord to send me became a long and drawn-out process. Having little patience, I turned to my move to Oregon for hopes of a better life. It was February 1, and I had just moved into a home in the rural area of Beaverton. This was exciting, because a friend told me about a couple who needed someone to watch their home rent-free for six months.

They were going on an extended vacation and wanted a reliable person to take care of their house and animals. Thinking this was a blessing from the Lord, I accepted the job and moved into my new territory and a new house at the same time.

God had shown me earlier in the year that He was going to do a wonderful thing in my life, and I would be in Oregon when He fulfilled His promise. Being a little desperate for a blessing, I called out to the Lord. I cried out, "When, God, when are You going to bless me?" Immediately after I said these words, the Lord spoke to me audibly.

I heard a loud and commanding voice in my right ear. He answered, "February or March." I thought moving to Oregon was the beginning of this promise, because I arrived February 1 and was now living in the right place. Putting these two things together, I was sure this was what I had been waiting for. As it turned out, however, this was most definitely not the blessing.

Moving to Beaverton turned out to be a horrible decision. The house I moved into had an eerie feeling to it from day one. The owners may have been Satan worshipers, because they had voodoo dolls, strange crystals, and all sorts of perverted, demonic statues.

The very first night I stayed in the house I had the most grotesque dream ever. This started a nightly ritual that was to continue the whole time I was there. Many nights I would have bad dreams, only to wake up and actually see demons in my room. I slept with the lights on each night and could only sleep for short periods of time before waking to pray. This was no blessing—it was a trap. I couldn't find another place to live because the people had a dog and two goats to tend. I did some checking and found they had no relatives close by to take over for me, so I was truly stuck. For six months I endured things I can't write about.

Even though the enemy was attacking daily, the Lord kept visiting me in dreams and visions. It was during those dark days in Beaverton that the Lord was to give me supernatural revelation in the form of "scripture dreams." Scripture dreams are vivid visions and dreams that can be found written in God's Word the Bible. This next dream turned out to be a fantastic visual picture of the Second Coming of Christ. Here is the dream/vision as I received it.

After praying for a good night's rest, I found myself in a spectacular dream that proved to be an exact picture of two separate scriptures tied together by God. In this powerful dream I was going to see my first visual picture of the return of our Lord and Savior Jesus Christ.

In this dream I was walking on the most unusual highway I had ever seen. It was straight as an arrow and about three lanes wide. The shocking thing about this particular highway was that it was made of crystal-clear water. This startled me; I looked down to see that I was walking on this liquid highway without sinking. The water was so pure and clear that words cannot describe its beauty; it sparkled like diamonds.

At this point I looked around to see others walking with me on this strange road that led to who knows where. I knew that everyone walking on this heavenly highway was saved— not one unbeliever was in sight. As I looked around, I could see some of my Christian friends following just behind me. Looking back, my eyes fixed on my longtime friend Pearl Penning. She was leaping and rejoicing, and when her eyes met mine we spoke to each other mind to mind. Our mouths didn't move at all, and yet words were being transmitted in the spirit. This is what she said to me: "This is it; this is what we have been waiting for."

This seemed miraculous to me for two reasons: First, Pearl has multiple sclerosis and cannot walk very well. In this dream she was totally healed from head to foot. I was full of joy knowing that God had healed her. Not only that, we were speaking to each other in a way not humanly possible. We were connected in the spirit, I guessed, as I marveled at this new experience.

Suddenly, I saw my friend Nick in my mind's eye. He was in some other city or state, but I could see him as if he was standing a foot in front of me. Our minds were connected, and we seemed to be thinking with one mind. I knew every thought he had, and he knew my thoughts. As Nick and I connected up, I realized that something had just happened in America. I was not allowed to remember what it was, but I sensed it was a miracle of biblical proportion. I also knew the whole world was going to hear about this great event.

Just then I heard a loud trumpet blast coming down from above. I was startled, because the sound was right above me and was very powerful. I quickly ducked down as my instincts took over. Realizing I was OK, I looked up to see a most unusual sight. What appeared to be a cup and saucer came straight down from heaven and stopped in front of me at eye level.

I knew something was inside the cup, and I was compelled to lean forward to see what was hidden inside. Inside was a beautiful piece of bread. It was unlike any bread I had ever seen. It was more compact than the bread we Americans eat, and it looked like a small cake of sorts. It was perfectly square and gently rose at the top in the shape of a dome, making this unusual loaf of bread look like a heavenly temple.

Immediately I knew this bread represented Jesus. I also understood that I was seeing a picture of His imminent return to this planet. Before I finished processing all of this, the scene changed. Suddenly I was standing in front of a large mirror. Looking in this mirror, I realized that I looked older. My best guess is that I was 55 to 60 years old. (I had this vision in September of 1990; I was 32 at the time.) I had gotten the impression that God was showing me about how old I would be when Jesus returns for His bride, the church.

Waking from this vision I was filled with awe knowing I had been shown the Lord's return. Later I discovered this dream to be a visual picture of two separate scriptures.

I have received many of these living pictures out of God's Word and know it would be impossible to have a chance dream and then find it written in the Bible. Having had several of these supernatural visions since the first one, I have become a fanatic defender of God's Word.

A month later I was driving to a meeting with a local customer. I was listening to the Christian radio station as usual when suddenly I heard the radio preacher talking about a "highway that only Christians could walk on." I was shocked. I knew the heavenly highway dream was from the Lord, but discovering scriptures that described it filled me with awe.

I began listening with complete attention as this man preached about this highway mentioned in the Old Testament. I missed the beginning part where he gave the chapter and verse so I listened to his every word, hoping that he would give a clue as to where I could find this in the Bible.

Just as the program ended, the announcer told the audience that he had been reading out of the book on Isaiah but didn't say where. I ran to my Bible that night and began searching to find the confirming scriptures. I was amazed to find that a portion of my dream came directly out of this Old Testament book. It took quite a lot of reading (thirty-four chapters, in fact), but I finally found what I was looking for. "Say to them that are of a fearful heart, Be strong, fear not: behold, your God will come with vengeance, even God with a recompence; he will come and save you. Then the eyes of the blind shall be opened, and the ears of the deaf shall be unstopped. Then shall the lame leap as a hart and the tongue of the dumb sing: for in the wilderness shall waters break out, and streams in the desert. And the parched ground shall become a pool, and the thirsty land springs of water: in the habitation of dragons, where each lay, shall be grass with reeds and rushes. And a highway shall be there, and a way, and it shall be called The way of holiness; the unclean shall not pass over it; but it shall be for those: the wayfaring men, though fools, shall not err therein" (Isaiah 35:4-8).

This is exactly what I had seen in the dream. I had so many worries back then, and God was saying do not fear, for He shall come and save us. This is what the descending bread was all about. It was Jesus coming back. "And the lame shall leap" was illustrated by seeing Pearl leaping and running and praising the Lord. There will be a highway there, a way of holiness, and it is only for God's children. The unclean shall not pass over it. Isn't God awesome?

Shortly after that, God inspired me to open my Bible. I flipped it open, and these words seemed to jump off the page: "And Jesus said unto them, I am the bread of life: he that cometh to me shall never hunger; and he that believeth on me shall never thirst. The Jews then murmured at him, because he said, I am the bread which came down from heaven" (John 6:35, 44).

Another wonderful revelation is the cup coming down out of heaven. At the Last Supper the scripture puts it this way: "Jesus took the cup, and gave thanks and gave it to them saying, 'Drink from it all of you. For this is My blood of the covenant, which is shed for many for the remission of sins'" (Matthew 26:27-28 NKJV).

One other revelation has to do with the trumpet blast that I heard before seeing the cup descend. I was a new believer when I had this dream. I had a very limited understanding of God's Word and had never read the Old Testament. The revelation of this dream's meaning came to me slowly over the next few years.

It is amazing how you can hear someone preach from the Bible and miss what God is trying to say to you at that time. I found the highway of holiness reference a year or two after having this dream, but it took years for me to stumble on the fullness of this message from above.

Years later I was reading Thessalonians and found these confirming words: "For the Lord Himself will descend from heaven with a shout, with the voice of an archangel, with the 'trumpet of God'" (1 Thessalonians 4:16 NKJV).

So here is a wonderful picture of our Lord's return for His bride, the church. What a wonderful and heart-changing event! God was truly speaking to me in these dreams and visions, and He had a good reason to do so. I was unaware that I would later write these visions in a book, so I thanked God for the messages and shared them with as many people as I could.

I was convinced God was showing me dreams right out of His Word. Three separate times in the gospel of John, Jesus refers to Himself as bread coming down from heaven. After finding these scriptures, I began to wonder what God wanted me to do with all this information.

I was a baby Christian, and I knew I needed to mature and grow in the grace and the knowledge of God. Even so, I couldn't help feeling that God had a special reason for giving me these visions. I spent many hours pondering the meaning of life and wondering what I needed to do with the visions, if anything.

I kept asking God how He could use a wretch like me. I knew I wasn't completely right with Him, and I longed to walk clean before the Lord. Even in my foolishness, my wretched condition didn't seem to bother the Lord. He continued pouring out His Spirit and giving me new visions from above. Knowing my heart's cry for deliverance, God sent me the following dream in which He promised me a new heart and spirit.

I fell asleep after praying for protection from the evil that was present in the house I was watching in Beaverton. After falling asleep, I immediately found myself in another dream from the Lord. In this dream I awoke to see myself standing at attention, shoulders up and hands at my side. I remember thinking I looked like a soldier, and I was viewing myself as in a mirror. Suddenly a hand appeared out of nowhere. It was the same basic size and shape as my own hand, except you could see right through it.

It appeared right in front of me and was floating chest high about a foot away from my body. Before I could even think, the hand began to move. It went inside my chest where my heart is located, and at the same time I heard God speaking in my right ear. I also understood that it was His hand reaching inside my chest. These are the words He spoke: "My son, I am going to give you the heart of a child." Then the scene changed.

Once again I found myself viewing my body as if I was a soldier. I seemed to be about ten feet away, and the hand of God appeared again. It was at eye level and within reaching distance of my body. As I watched, God's hand moved up to my left eye and replaced it with a new one. I watched this happen in total silence and did not hear the Lord speak. This left me confused and wondering why I might need a new left eye. The dream ended with me standing there perplexed and confused.

I prayed many times for the interpretation to this unusual dream and got no answers. I knew it was a heavenly vision, but I had no Bible reference to decipher the message. It took about two months of waiting and a lot of prayer before the Lord would reveal the meaning of this dream to me. This is how He made sure that I understood the message.

I had taken a couple of days off and decided to head home to Tacoma and see my family and friends. After the usual hellos, I went to the mall to see Nick. We had a lot to discuss concerning the dreams God had been giving us, and we both felt the excitement that godly revelation brings. Knowing that I was staying for the weekend, Nick asked if

I would like to go hear a man tell his story about bringing the Russian Jews back to their homeland, Israel. This man had had written a book that chronicled his efforts. He was to give an update on his efforts during a church service. This sounded interesting, so I accepted Nick's invitation, and off we went.

As the man poured out his heart, I could tell that he loved the Lord. He had a conviction that came directly from God to bring the Jews out of Russia into their homeland. Before he discussed this exodus, He wanted to bring us a word from the Lord. That is when I felt God's Spirit in my heart, and I realized He had brought me to this church for a specific reason.

The guest speaker started preaching about people who are called of God but have not yet been sent out into the harvest field. My spiritual ears perked up, because this was the position I felt I was in. He then said that before God was going to use a person, He had to give him a new heart for service. To make his point he went to the Old Testament and preached about the Ammonites who came against the men at Jabesh-gilead. Apparently the Ammonites were much too great in number to fight against, so the men of Ja'besh said they would make a covenant with the Ammonites to serve them.

Knowing they were able to defeat the men at Ja'besh, the Ammonites agreed to this covenant with one stipulation—they wanted the men to gouge out their right eye as a sign of this treaty. Here is the scripture that was quoted: "And Nahash the Ammonite answered them, 'On this condition will I make a covenant with you, that I may thrust out all your right eyes, and lay it for a reproach upon all Israel'" (1 Samuel 11:2).

The speaker continued by asking the audience this question, "Why would the Ammonites want to thrust out the right eyes of the men at Ja'besh?" I was asking myself the very same thing when this man of God answered the question for us. He said that the right eye represented their spiritual vision. By gouging out their right eyes they were, in effect, taking away their vision for God.

The Bible states: "Where there is no vision, the people perish: but he that keepeth the law, happy is he" (Proverbs 29:18).

That is when he pointed out into the audience and proclaimed, "God wants to use some of you in a powerful way, but before he can do that, He has to give you a new heart and a new right eye." As soon as he said this, I was instantly back in the vision. I could see God's hand replacing the eye on my left side. I then realized I was looking at myself as in a mirror, so things were reversed. It looked as if I was receiving a new left eye, when in fact it was my right eye.

Immediately, Nick began exclaiming, "That's your vision! That's your vision!" I was stunned beyond words. This was truly a divine appointment. That day I received the interpretation explaining the vision's meaning. If I hadn't heard this sermon, it would have been impossible for me to understand the true meaning behind this unusual message from above.

Two months later as I was flipping through the Bible, I noticed this scripture. "A new heart also will I give you, and a new spirit will I put within you: and I will take away the stony heart out of your flesh, and I will give you an heart of flesh" (Ezekiel 36:26). This passage in Ezekiel was an exact picture of my vision.

God proved to me once again that the Bible is His true and living Word. Shortly after this, I had a third scripture dream that offered an awesome promise for those who serve God.

In this dream I was standing by a shoreline, looking out over the horizon, when a man suddenly appeared at my right side. He said, "Scott, I am going to take you to the secret place that no man can find." With that, he took me up in the sky. As we went up, I could see dark clouds, and then we entered total darkness. It was so dark that I heard my voice say, "No one can find us in this place." All at once I could see again, and I then realized that we were still up in the air. I looked down to see channels of water running in the same direction. It looked like rows of water canals in between strips of land that were covered with lush forests. I remember thinking that it looked like the place where time began, but that was only an impression I had at the time.

Then the scene changed. All at once we were standing on the bank of one of these unusual channels, in front of a bridge that led to the other side. That is when this man spoke again. "Scott, do you see this bridge? It was built at great expense, but when they built it they forgot the proper foundation." When he said this, a foundation appeared on the right side of the bridge, and then as quickly as it appeared, it was gone. This foundation represented the true and living words written in God's Word. It represented the true gospel of Christ, which had been diluted and changed by evil men. The bridge represented the church.

He continued speaking: "Because they forgot the proper foundation, no car can cross this bridge. If a car tries to cross to the other side, the bridge will sink, and all will be lost." Then my ears were stopped up so I could not remember what was said. I watched as his lips moved, but I could not hear one single word he was saying. I remember knowing that God wanted to seal up the words that were spoken.

At this point the scene changed again. We were suddenly standing in front of what looked like a huge water valve. I also noticed a small valve in the center of the larger one. At this point, the man began opening the floodgates by turning the large valve. When he had finished, he said something to me that I wasn't allowed to remember, and I began turning the small valve in the center.

I wasn't sure why we were opening the valves, but I got the feeling that we were flooding the bridge to prevent cars from trying to cross. I also had the impression that a new bridge was going to be built. This is my interpretation only, as God has kept silent on this subject.

With that I woke from this complicated vision. I lay in bed wondering what it might mean. Somehow I knew that God was going to show me, so I turned my attention toward God and began thanking Him for giving me these strange dreams.

Three months later, I was taking my usual Saturday afternoon nap when I found myself looking down on a policeman as he was driving his car. I could see inside the car, and I noticed that he was wearing black gloves as he drove down the highway.

As soon as I saw the gloves, I knew what he was up to. He was driving around looking for Christians. I also knew why he was looking for God's children; the police were hunting down Christians for detention. I got the feeling that they had plans to put us away for good.

Then I was in my own car driving down the road. I was trying to find a certain church or a building where I knew my brothers in Christ were hiding. I had a fearful feeling inside me, and I longed to find this place of refuge. That is when I heard God say, "My son, you have to go to Psalm 18. Find Psalm 18."

I immediately woke from my sleep and, still shocked at this dream, I got out of bed to get my Bible. As soon as my feet hit the floor, I heard these words almost shouted in my right ear: "Psalm 18!" I grabbed my Bible, and for the first time ever I read from the book of Psalms.

Psalm 18 read like a review of my life. King David wrote many psalms, and at this point he must have felt exactly the way I did as he wrote about his life. Listen to how he starts this psalm: "The Lord is my Rock, and my fortress and my deliverer; my God, my strength." This caught my attention because of my dream about the rock. Then David continues: "The sorrows of hell compassed me about: the snares of death prevented me." This is exactly how I was feeling because of my stressful life and the demon-possessed home I was tending.

Then David wrote: "In my distress I called unto my God: He heard my voice out of His Temple." Then God came and delivered David out of the hand of the enemy. He also made him the head of the heathen, and they served and feared David because of God. This was a special promise that God was going to save me. As I was reading through this beautiful psalm, I found some passages that explain the meaning to the dream I had two months before. Examine these passages, and then judge for yourself: "God made darkness His secret place" (verse 11); "Yea, He sent out His arrows and scattered them; and He shot out lightnings, and discomforted them. Then the channels of waters were seen, and the foundations of the world were discovered at thy rebuke, O Lord" (verses 14-15).

I was convinced that this last dream was a living picture of Psalm 18. Even the order in which the dream came to me was correct according to God's Word. I believe God was saying that He knew exactly where I was in life and was going to help me and bless me even though the gates of hell compassed about my life. He will also save all those who put their trust in Him just as He promised and this is truly good news for all that believe.

With three scripture dreams in six months, I was getting a practical lesson on the validity of God's Word. Through these dreams, God's Word came to life before my very eyes. I now know that God used these dreams to get me to trust the Bible as His living Word. At this point I was unaware that I was about to go through some very troubled waters. I was going to need this great faith to get me through the time of testing and I thank God for His promise to keep us through the fire and flood.

♦ 9 ♦

Down in the Valley with Jesus

This chapter is dedicated to all the times I was honored to see Jesus. In my Christian walk I have seen Him many times and in different ways. In my first vision of Jesus, I saw Him as the rock. After that, I had a magnificent vision of Jesus in the form of a fish. He then appeared as bread coming down from heaven.

In my next encounters with the Lord, I was allowed to see Jesus the way we normally think of Him—in His body. These encounters always fill my heart with great joy and hope, knowing that no matter how hard life may get, the Lord is there and will see us through until the day of salvation.

The first time I saw the Lord was the most spectacular and shocking event of my life. I was still tending the house in Beaverton. Little did I know that in two weeks I was going to have a breakdown that would change the course of my life.

It was now August 1991. It had been a long summer, filled with sorrow, as I endured severe depression during the day and unbelievable fear at night. I was slipping into darkness. If the Lord hadn't intervened, I might not have made it through to today.

I had gone to bed as usual and was in prayer asking God to protect me from the enemy attacks that were so frequent. As I tried to sleep, something started to happen that was to continue for three nights. As I closed my eyes, the power of God came floating down to surround me.

Lying there with God's power moving through me, I began to pray in the Spirit for what seemed to be a full hour. I was not used to praying for that duration and felt that these prayers were powerful and specific. Not knowing what I was praying since I was praying in tongues, I lay there wondering who or what I might be praying for.

As I tried to sleep, it happened again. Down came God's power, and off I went in the Spirit, praying as I had never prayed before. This kept up all night long; it would be 4 a.m. before God would let me sleep.

The next night this happened again, and I cried out for God to let me sleep as His power kept pouring through me. I watched the clock pass 4 a.m. before I felt a release and was able to sleep.

The third night came, and by 10 p.m. I felt I was going to get some rest. I prayed and asked God to please let me sleep, as I was unable to do my job in this exhausted state. At 11 p.m., my eyes began to close, and I started to slip into a dream state.

A minute later God's power fell again. Instantly, my eyes were wide open. I cried out for relief as I begged God to let me sleep, but the power kept coming and seemed to increase to a new level of anointing than I had ever felt. I began praying in the Spirit, and this time I could feel the power of the prayers coming out of my mouth. These were no ordinary prayers. All prayers are beautiful, but I knew these powerful prayers were being felt somewhere on this earth or in the spirit world.

This kept up all night. I was so filled with God's power that I lost all track of time. This continued until 3 a.m. As

I was praying, a burst of supernatural power came flowing down from above, and with it came an audible command from God: "Ask Jesus to come." Before my mind caught up with my ears, a burst of power came from deep inside me, forcing the following words out of my mouth: "Come, Lord Jesus."

I knew that the Holy Spirit inside me had responded before I had a chance to think. I had the TV and bedroom lights on, and immediately after these words were spoken, a power surge moved through the house. This surge was so intense that the lights flickered and the TV screen went blank for a split second.

That is when I realized that Jesus was standing right in front of my bed. In the twinkling of an eye, He had appeared. He was standing about five feet away and His arms were outstretched the way you see in so many depictions of Him.

He was wearing a beautiful, sparkling-white robe that was so brilliant it looked as if it was glowing with heavenly perfection. As I looked on, I noticed His robe was laden with gold. This heavenly garment had a golden hem. I could barely see the Lord's toes, because His robe flowed all the way down to the floor.

I then noticed that His cuffs and neckline were trimmed with golden stitching that looked as if it was made for a king. Across His chest He wore a beautiful solid-gold sash. This golden sash covered his upper body completely, as it criss-crossed His chest. The overall look reminded me of something you would see on an ancient Egyptian king. This golden sash shone with a heavenly sparkle. It bore a flowing design that looked like the feathers on the wings of an eagle.

As I examined this beautiful garment, I suddenly could see right through the sleeves of His robe. That is when I saw how powerful and beautiful His arms were. The Bible says that He was raised in power, and the Lord let me see just how mighty He really is. These were no ordinary arms—they were mighty arms and had the look of heavenly perfection.

As I examined His arms, power was flowing from the Lord that went right through my being like little bolts of lightning. I began to shake all over and cry out as I could see my hopelessly sinful nature compared to the holiness of the Lord. That is what happens to a person in the presence of God—you are stripped naked with no place to hide. At this point I began to plead with the Lord to leave.

As a river of tears poured out of my eyes, I kept saying, "I'm not worthy! I'm not worthy!" I was truly in the presence of God. I pleaded with Him to leave, and the Lord disappeared without a word. After that, I sat in total silence as tears kept flowing from my eyes. I was an emotional wreck. I was tired, confused, and scared. What did this mean? Why did Jesus visit me? Why didn't He say something? He could have said hello, or goodbye, or how are you. Anything would have been better than nothing. Come to think of it, I didn't even get to see His face, leaving me all the more confused.

I lay there for what seemed to be a couple of hours before falling asleep. The whole time, the Holy Spirit was moving through me like oil. At one point it felt as if God was strumming my electrons, because I could feel a vibration in my body, and it seemed to flow like a song. I am not sure why the Lord did this to me, but I am telling it anyway to give you the whole picture of what happened.

The next morning I was very emotional. I canceled my appointments for the day, not caring what the buyers would say. I needed to think, and quite frankly, I didn't care if my sales territory sank into the ocean.

I decided to call my friend Nick and tell him what had just happened. I wasn't sure if he would be at work, but I took a chance and called there anyway. The phone rang once, and Nick picked it up. We hadn't talked for at least three months, so he was surprised to hear my voice.

He then told me that it was a miracle I called when I did, because it was his day off, and the Lord impressed on his mind to go in to work. He thought he might have forgotten something important and the Lord was prompting him to go in to take care of things. He was also shocked because just as he walked into his department, the phone rang once, and he was right there to pick it up.

He then asked me why I had called him at work. Suddenly a flood of emotion came to the surface of my being. I started to cry, and I heard Nick saying, "Are you OK? Is everything all right?" All I could say was, "Jesus came to my home last night." Then, without waiting for a response, I hung up the phone.

This may sound like a strange thing to do, but I was a wreck. As I told Nick what had happened to me, I also felt an arrow of doubt pierce my heart. I went through a list of things that might have happened: I dreamed it, or I imagined it, or I was out of my mind, and so forth.

I began to cry and started saying out loud, "They're not going to believe me! They're not going to believe me!" Then I heard God speak: "My son, get your Bible, and I will confirm it in My Word."

Shaking badly, I rushed to get my Bible. I sat on the sofa and quickly said this simple prayer: "Dear Lord, please show me in Your Word that Jesus came to visit me last night." With that, I closed my eyes and opened up my Bible. I kept my eyes shut and put my finger on the spot I knew God wanted me to see. This is where it landed: "Hear the right, O Lord, attend unto my cry, give ear unto my prayer, that goeth not out of feigned lips. Let my sentence come forth from thy presence; let thine eyes behold the things that are equal. Thou hast proved mine heart; Thou hast visited me in the night; thou hast tried me, and shalt find nothing; I am purposed [that] my mouth shall not transgress" (Psalm 17:1-3).

Seeing these words felt as miraculous as seeing Jesus. There is no way this could be by chance. I knew that I had seen the Lord, and now with this confirming scripture, I could defend this event with all the faith in the world. I spent the rest of the day thanking God for His favor and wondering why He was spending so much time on a wretch like me.

I still do not know the full scope of what happened that night. I do know that after He appeared in my room, the house was swept clean of any and all demonic activity. From that point on the house was so spiritually clean that I used the word "sterile" to describe how it felt.

Two weeks after this wonderful event, I had a breakdown that turned the course of my life. I had been running my whole life—running from my past wounds, running from my fears, running from becoming who I really needed to be. I found out you can run, but you cannot hide. Exhausted from a life of turmoil, my emotional legs gave out.

I came home one night after a very stressful day, and I lost it. I burst out crying. It hurt so bad I thought I was going to die. I was through running. I could run no farther, so I had little choice. The next day I called my boss to give my two-week notice. I explained my situation to him, and he was very understanding and wished me well in whatever I decided to do.

I had already arranged to move back with my folks. Thank God for my beautiful parents. Without their love and support, I may not have made it. With those arrangements made, all I had to do was wait until the owners of the home came back, and I was free to leave my old life behind to find the person I needed to be.

Before I knew it, the owners of the house called to tell me they were one day away from returning. Wanting to get out of that horrible place, I fed the animals, and off I went. As I headed north to Tacoma, I wondered what was on the other side of tomorrow. I was totally broken. Little did I know that

I would spend the next four years living at my parents' house while God rebuilt me from the inside out.

Moving back home was painful indeed. In the four seasons' scenario, this would definitely be winter. In this case it was going to be the longest winter ever recorded. Powerless to do anything about my broken condition, I lay down in the hands of God for a time of healing.

I spent the next four years living in the back bedroom of my parents' home. The first two years all I did was mourn and grieve as I worked through the hidden wounds in my heart. The next two years were times of rebuilding and spiritual growth. It was during these four years that God showed me things that not many people see. May God bless my parents for loving me enough to endure the pain as they shared the hardship of my broken life.

I had a lot of healing to do. I couldn't work because I was too broken to function. This was my wilderness experience, and I knew it was going to be painful. At that time I didn't understand that God uses these hardships to birth in us a new heart. God had allowed this situation to come into my life to make me, not to break me. I needed a whole new foundation, and God wanted it to be Jesus.

As I made it from day to day, I began to see God sustaining me in what looked like a hopeless situation. This began to give me great peace, because I realized that it was the Lord's responsibility to take care of His own, and I got to see many financial and personal miracles that proved God was holding me up.

As I worked through the wounds of life, I began to understand the purpose of suffering. I started to see the necessity of the hard times and realized that God used these things to knock off the rough edges that keep us from living life to its fullest potential. As I looked deeper into God's Word I found an amazing number of scriptures that confirmed this point.

During those days of discovery I began to see God molding me and shaping me into a new creation. It was truly painful, but I accepted the situation, knowing my suffering was necessary for spiritual growth. Shortly after coming to this revelation, my friends and family began to think God had something against me. They didn't mind telling me so, and this subject came up all the time. I have to admit that things looked pretty bad in the natural.

I tried to keep this in mind whenever the subject came up. I avoided discussing the subject. I didn't blame them for feeling the way they did, because my life was truly a mess. To the natural man, suffering is not a sign of blessing, and I found out that many preachers of the Word also have this mindset. Some teach that a man found in my sad situation either lacks faith or is being judged by God.

They wound a lot of good people by this teaching, and the end results can be confusion and shame to the suffering saint. The Lord is not pleased with this false teaching because it furthers the affliction of His children by declaring their suffering to be God's judgment. Having come to a new understanding on this subject, I had peace in my heart. I knew God was using my hard times to change and cleanse me. The problems of life and the pressures of the day were part of God's healing and necessary for me to become the man that God intended me to be.

God does judge sin, for He is a holy God who cannot tolerate the sinful acts of the flesh. I did need judging, so I accepted the hard times, knowing I was guilty as charged. But I found out that God had a higher purpose in allowing my suffering. He was trying to teach me to live by faith. The Bible says, "Now faith is the substance of things hoped for, the evidence of things not seen" (Hebrews 11:1). If you hope for something, you don't have it yet; if it is not seen, then it will be revealed later. The Christian reward is yet to come, and it is an eternal reward. Abraham, the father of our faith, understood this truth and proved it by the way he lived.

The Bible states, "By faith Abraham, when he was called to go out into a place which he should after receive for an inheritance, obeyed; and he went out, not knowing whither he went. By faith he sojourned in the land of promise, as [in] a strange country, dwelling in tabernacles with Isaac and Jacob, the heirs with him of the same promise: for he looked for a city which hath foundations, whose builder and maker [is] God" (Hebrews 11:9).

Abraham and his sons lived in the land God had given them as if they did not possess it. Instead of building a great city, they lived in tents. They did this because they were looking for a city that was built by God—one that would last forever.

God wanted to teach me this way of living, and it was painful to learn. He also wanted to assure me that He would be my helper and healer. One morning as I woke, I heard God's audible voice. He said: "The just shall live by faith." I was so sick at the time I just rolled over and said, "God, I am too weak; You will have to help me." Immediately upon saying this, I had an open-eyed vision.

I saw the body of Christ in a state of total confusion. We were all going around in circles like dogs chasing their tails. Then I felt the breath of God come down from heaven. This breath was powerful and spun us all like tops. I watched as we spun and spun. Suddenly we all stopped and were lined up in a perfect row. Each person was in the exact and correct place, and we were all healed. I looked up to heaven and thanked the Lord for His healing as this vision faded from my mind's eye.

It took me a while to learn to trust God in all things. Even in the midst of the storm, God's arm is not shortened that He cannot save us. He can heal our land whenever He decides to. Meanwhile, the troubles we face test us to see if we have genuine faith, and the hardships refine us as gold is made pure through the fire. After being tested and approved, we can be confident that He will take us to heaven and give us an eternal reward for our faithfulness.

Jesus declared this truth many times and in various ways. He spoke about His rewards and declared His heavenly kingdom in many scriptures. Jesus said: "My kingdom is not of this world" (John 18:36). And again: "Behold, I come quickly; and my reward is with Me, to give every man according as his work shall be" (Revelation 22:12).

By this knowledge I can have joy. I know that whatever comes my way, I have the hope set before me that God will come and do away with suffering and sorrow. I can't seem to figure out why so many pastors preach otherwise. They seem to be preaching blessings, prosperity, and health. I had a hard time holding fast to the concept of suffering because the church is supposed to represent God but was preaching just the opposite.

However, the Lord showed me the truth about living by faith, and He confirmed that I was on the right track through the following vision of Jesus.

For some time I had been wondering about the things God had been showing me. I had only two choices: either God was on my side and was taking me through this hard time for a specific reason, or He was mad at me and was punishing me for my sinful deeds. Knowing my thoughts, God confirmed to me that I had His blessings by giving me another dream of Jesus.

In this dream I was walking around on what looked like a golf course that had no greens. The grass in this vision seemed to be perfect in color, size, and shape. As I looked around, I saw men scouring the grass. I knew without a question that they were looking for Jesus. Then God let me see some men gather in a little area over by some trees that lined this unusual grass field. Then I saw another group of men standing in a circle around the top of a little hill in the middle of this beautiful grass concourse. Suddenly, with telescopic vision I could see both groups of men as if I was in their midst. I then got to see what they had found and what they were looking at.

Looking down with these heavenly eyes, I saw boiling tar pits where the men had gathered. I could see the pitch-black tar as it bubbled from the heat within. I knew this black tar represented the doctrines of demons, and I knew the men thought they had found what they had been looking for, but they were deceived.

Suddenly, I saw Jesus walking up to me. He had a small group of men with Him and was now coming to get me. I had found the Lord, or should I say He found me. The men with Him were full of joy, and I knew Jesus had called and chosen us all.

Jesus turned and looked directly at me. I looked into His heavenly eyes, and they were so beautiful I thought I would melt. They looked like laser beams, and I knew He could see right into my soul. He then spoke to me and said, "Come and follow Me. I am going to take you to a place that you have never been, and I'm going to show you things that you know not." When these words reached my ears I could feel love like a peaceful river. I felt like the most important person in His kingdom. Jesus really loves me, and I could feel His love as it moved through my heart. The wonderful thing is that He turned to talk to the rest of the men, and I knew they too felt this same special love. After that, Jesus turned and began leading us to who knows where. I only knew that I was allowed to go with Him, and I realized how undeserving I was to even be called by His name.

Waking from this encouraging dream, I felt total joy. I knew God had given me this dream to let me know I was on the right track. What I still didn't get was how God could use a weak person like me to do His bidding. What I have since learned is that God chooses weak people on purpose. He wants it that way so people will know that it's God's power that gets the victory and not our own.

Almost immediately I had another vision that was the most awesome yet. God wanted me to see that His son, Jesus, secured the victory over Satan when He rose from the grave. This is great news because if we are found in Jesus, we too have that victory along with our Lord and Savior Jesus Christ.

While I was sleeping, I was in what I thought was a vision of the endtime ministry of the saints. I looked around to see groups of roving people looking for food and shelter. I was standing by the edge of a grass cliff looking down at a field of grass that started at the bottom of the cliff, when a group of people suddenly surrounded me.

The leader of this group walked up to me and said, "If your God is really God, throw these darts down this hill. If all the darts land inside the circle we will know your God truly is God, but if any of these darts land outside the circle, we will know that your God is not God." As I looked on, a perfect circle appeared at the bottom of this cliff. The circle was formed by a two-inch thick line and was about six feet in diameter. The line that formed the circle was whiter than anything I had ever seen. After that a box full of three-inch long darts appeared at my feet.

Suddenly, a burst of God's power came pouring down from above, and instantly I had the might of Samson as I bent down to grab the box of darts. I had a confidence that can only come from the Lord. I threw the whole box of darts with the flick of my wrists. I didn't even aim for the circle. In fact, I had to throw the darts behind my back because I was facing the other way.

Instantly the scene changed. We were now standing at the bottom of the hill just to the side of the circle. As I watched, my eyes beheld something that can best be described as the finger of God. The first dart came down from above with heavenly perfection, with absolutely zero vibration. It hit its mark with the smoothest perfection. It also seemed to be propelled by some power, because it landed with the speed of an arrow shot from a bow. When it landed I knew it was the Lord's dart, and it landed inside the circle to the right.

Soon another landed in ordinary fashion inside the circle to the left. Then everything froze just long enough for me to see that these two darts were on opposite sides of the circle. I had the impression that they were opposing one another.

After that, the rest of the darts fell like a thousand shooting arrows. Some kind of spiritual power was separating the darts in mid-air. They all landed inside the circle, some to the left side and some to the right.

When they landed, they hit smack dab on top of each other. One after the other they stacked to the height of a man. They then built outward, forming a solid mass like a column. When all the darts had landed, the two columns seemingly came alive and formed into two statues. The column to the right formed into Jesus, and the column to the left formed into Satan.

I was taken back by the exquisite detail. Each statue was gray and was so perfect that a master artist's best sculpture would pale in comparison. I knew they were not of this earth.

I understood what was happening. Jesus and Satan were standing face-to-face, looking at each other as if they were ready to do battle. Their faces were set like a flint, and their eyes were fixed like a hawk's. They were leaning in toward each other.

That is when my eyes focused on what the Lord wanted me to see.

Satan had a dagger in his right hand, and he had thrust it into Jesus' side. He planted the dagger in the same spot that was pierced when Jesus hung on the cross. Jesus also had a dagger in His right hand. Jesus had taken His dagger and plunged it into Satan's right temple. I then heard a voice coming down from above, proclaiming: "It's the deathblow."

I knew immediately what these words meant. Jesus gave Satan the final blow—the deathblow. The people began shouting, "Jesus has won! Jesus has won!" After this, the statues started to move. I could see the cement-like substance start to ripple like water. In seconds, the statues came alive, and immediately Satan was taken away. He was pulled away by an invisible force to the left of my field of vision and disappeared out of sight. Jesus then went up towards heaven, and in the twinkling of an eye He was gone. After that, the Holy Spirit came flooding down and filled me with unstoppable and unmovable power. I was instantly transformed from the inside out, and all my human fears were wiped away.

Just then, I saw a multitude of people that I could not count coming at me. They were drawn by the power of God and wanted healing and deliverance. The people formed a wedge, and a woman in front was holding a little girl's hand that was defective from birth. Having God's power, I said, "I'm going to pray for that hand, and God is going to heal it." The woman replied, "No, you are not to do the healing—he is supposed to." She pointed behind me—and I looked to see my friend Nick.

With a godly jealously, I closed my eyes and shouted, "God, what do You want me to do?" I opened my eyes and beheld a sea of people before me. Filled with the Holy Spirit, I began to preach to them with boldness.

I have seen Jesus five times since this awesome vision. Each time He shows me a little more about His nature and plan for His children. I now know that the Lord is on His way back. That is why He showed Himself to me so many times. Part of His plan was that years later, He would have me write a book about these miraculous events. I believe that through reading this book, many will come to salvation, as they finally believe in the "King of kings and the Lord of lords, Jesus Christ."

♦ 10 ♦

God Signs with His Blood

In 1992 God let me see something that no one to my knowledge has ever seen. He later told me it was a sign of a yet-to-be fulfilled visitation by God to the Pacific Northwest. God has confirmed these plans to me in many ways. God is about to do something in this area that the whole world is going to know about.

This event began in September of 1990. I was living in Tacoma and was about to move to Beaverton to take over the sales territory that covered the entire state. It was Friday night and, like most weekends, I was alone with nothing to do. Depleted by pressures too numerous to list, I headed for the liquor store seeking to shut off the pain. I knew I shouldn't drink, but I couldn't take the loneliness. I became depressed, and the overwhelming darkness turned to grief.

That night I sat at home and drank my way into a place where feelings don't count. About 3 a.m. I awoke feeling as if a truck had just run over my head. I was hurting; my body was sick and I knew I was out of control. I began asking God to forgive me and wondered how He could call me one of His own.

As I lay there in pain, I began to cry out to the Lord. As I cried out, God's power came pouring down like a flood. Instantly, my headache was gone, replaced with an overwhelming power so strong that I leaped out of bed and began to march back and forth in my bedroom. I started praying as I marched, and I kept this up for a good ten minutes. Finally, I felt a release in the spirit, and I jumped back in bed.

As soon as my head hit the pillow, I had an open-eyed vision from the Lord. I was in Oregon, running in place as if doing aerobics. I knew what this meant—God was going to quicken my spirit and He was going to do so in the state of Oregon. After having this insight, I saw a path heading due east, extending from Oregon to New York. I knew that whatever was going to happen to me in Oregon would be known across the country.

I asked out loud, "When will this be, God?" I heard God's voice: "February or March." His answer confused me. If God knows everything—and He does—then why wasn't He more precise? I thought at this point that I must have missed God or heard wrong. Not knowing what this meant, I turned it over to fate and went back to sleep.

Four months later I moved to Beaverton, to the unholy house I wrote about earlier, and started my new sales territory on February 1, 1991. I thought this was what I had been waiting for. I reasoned that God had said "February or March" because the timing of my move hinged on certain unstable events. As it turned out, this was not the blessing I had hoped for; I moved back to Tacoma and had to wait one more year for God to make good on His promise. It was well worth the wait, and then some.

It was now February 1992. I missed the fellowship with the friends I had made in Beaverton and tried to make every other prayer meeting at Lynn's house. We always had special times of prayer and fellowship in the Lord. I stayed with my good friend Bill, and this was a blessing as we caught up on current events in our lives and shared testimonies of God and His mighty works.

It was on one of these routine trips down to Oregon that God was going to show up in a way that would make my visit anything but routine.

One day while talking to Bill on the phone, I decided to go down and attend the next Bible study at Lynn's on February 27. Bill had invited me to stay at his house as usual. This made it nice, because all I had to do was show up with my Bible in hand and the rest of the details were taken care of. I was looking forward to this particular meeting because I had been fasting for several weeks and had an overwhelming feeling that the Lord was going to meet us in a special way.

I headed south on Interstate 5, which would take me the 150 miles to meet up with my friends. Tired from the physical drain that fasting can bring, I battled substantial fatigue as I drove the entire distance in monsoon-like rain squalls.

I was totally exhausted when I arrived and Bill suggested I lay down before we headed out for the night. Checking our watches we decided that I had an hour to rest, so I thanked Bill for his hospitality and headed up to the guest bedroom.

As I ascended the staircase I wondered what this night would bring. Every time I attended this all-night Bible study something powerful would happen. I had no clue that tonight I would experience the most powerful meeting in my entire Christian life.

God was going to do great things, and He started moving before we even got to Lynn's house. As I ascended the stairs, God spoke to me in that still soft voice I have come to love and know. I heard God say, "My son, I am able to give you a full night's rest in one hour if you ask me." I kept climbing the stairs while I silently asked God to give me a full night's rest in the hour I had to sleep.

It was 4 in the afternoon and almost dark outside. As I turned the room light out, I watched as the fading sunlight dimly illuminated my place of rest. As soon as my head hit the pillow the room became dark. I was startled because something dramatic had just happened. I had not yet slept, but I felt totally rested, and the room that was light a second ago was now dark.

Reaching for my watch, I looked towards the bedroom door. To my total amazement I looked,

and standing guard in front of my door was an angel of God. It was a huge angel who stood as high as the ceiling, with immense shoulders stretching wider than the doorway. He was wearing a white top that looked something like a sports jersey, and with his wide shoulders he almost looked like a football player. My eyes focused on the symbols on his chest. In the center of his chest was a lapis blue symbol that looked like two triangles joined together to form a diamond shape. On each arm he had a bright red symbol that looked like an hourglass made by connecting two triangles at their tips.

Here is a rendering of these symbols:

DIAGRAM OF ANGEL SYMBOLS

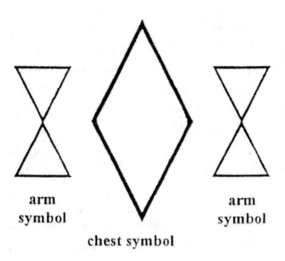

arm
symbol

arm
symbol

chest symbol

The diagram above depicts the Symbols on the angel's chest and Arms. The symbols on his arms were bright-red and the diamond shaped symbol on his chest was lapis-blue in color.

After I saw these symbols, the angel faded out of sight like a vapor. I leaped out of bed. I felt great. I felt so good that there was no doubt God had done just as He said. The amazing thing is that my watch showed that it was 5 p.m. Exactly one hour had passed in what seemed to be seconds. I ran downstairs to tell Bill, and we both rejoiced and knew God had a special night planned. This set our hearts to wondering what God had in store for us on this rainy Thursday night.

This night of miracles started as we began singing praise songs to the Lord. I started to feel the power of God swelling up inside me. I felt God's power filling me from the inside out, and my hands began to shake violently. Suddenly the spirit of prophecy came flooding down from above, and I found myself interrupting the song to prophesy to a person in the room. The power of God was so strong that I continued receiving words from heaven, and for three hours we prayed in the Spirit as God led us.

The power of God was so intense that my hands felt like magnets pulling me along as the Lord led me to one person after another to pray. Each time the Holy Spirit would bring to light hidden knowledge, and we were all convinced that God was speaking to us in a profound way. Bill was also praying alongside me, and together we witnessed many miracles as God poured out His Spirit on the people in the room.

Bill felt confident that right then and there, God would heal this one woman who had a broken neck. This was my first time ever praying for a physical healing, but I was filled with superhuman confidence. With great anticipation we headed for her chair and prepared to pray.

We were moved with compassion. This woman was in extreme pain. She had been in an accident that not only broke her neck but also left her in a metal cage around her head and chest that restricted her movements. Her obvious discomfort moved our hearts to seek God for an end to this suffering.

Nothing in my walk with God could have prepared me for what happened next. As Bill began to pray, the power of God came flooding down from above. I heard God's voice command me: "Put your right hand on her forehead and pray the words that I put in your mouth." I obeyed, and as I put my hand on her forehead words came to me that I know without question to be the very words of God: "Come, dear Jesus, and fill this vessel with Your healing power."

The power of God hit her like a ton of bricks. She straightened up with a force so violent that it threw her body up in the air. People standing nearby caught her as she landed with her head and shoulders on the seat of a chair. Her body and legs were sticking straight out, as stiff as a mummy.

Overwhelmed by God's power, she passed out and lay there as limp as a rag.

We were so filled with the Spirit of God that we turned and began praying for the next person without waiting for her to revive. God's power was so intense that our hands were tingling and seemed to be radiating the very power of the Holy Spirit. God continued to pour out His Spirit.

About ten minutes later I glanced over to see the woman with the broken neck sitting upright, with the glory of God resting on her. She was beaming with joy, and a light surrounding her face seemed to reflect the very presence of God. God had touched her and removed all her pain, leaving a supernatural feeling that the Bible calls joy unspeakable. God healed her that night, and soon after her doctor took a set of X-rays that proved it.

I had a tough time leaving the meeting that night. I was so filled with joy that I didn't want it to end. I remember thinking that nothing could top this night. Little did I know that two days later God had something planned that was going to redefine my understanding of exciting. God was getting ready to show me something that would fulfill the promise God had made to me two years earlier.

When we arrived back at Bill's, I realized I had left my glasses at Lynn's. Suddenly an overwhelming feeling came over me that God wanted me to go back to Lynn's for a specific reason that had nothing to do with my glasses. I began to wonder what He might have in mind and decided to call Lynn first thing in the morning to see when we could get together.

The next morning, Bill and I reflected on the miracles of the previous night. We couldn't help wondering what God had in store for us, and we were filled with anticipation as we looked forward to our next visit to Lynn's house.

I called Lynn to see if he had found my glasses. His wife Connie had found them, and he confessed that they felt God was going to do something with me when I came to get them. On Saturday morning, we headed over to Lynn's place in anticipation of God showing up for reasons unknown. When we arrived, we were filled with thanksgiving and began to worship God with everything in us.

It was time to pray. I started out praying for Lynn's son, and God's Holy Spirit was with me to bring words of encouragement to strengthen his Christian walk. After that, all eyes turned to me. It was my turn to get some prayer, and we were all excited, wondering what God might have in store for us.

I sat in the middle of the room, and everyone began to pray. With my eyes closed, I listened as Bill prayed God's blessings over me. All of a sudden, I saw a teardrop formed from the blood of Jesus. This was no vision; it was real. Don't ask me how this is possible, but with God, all things are possible.

I sat there with my eyes closed looking at this teardrop with 20/20 vision. It was so beautiful and such a bright red that I had to turn my head away as my eyes got used to its light. It was three-dimensional. I knew it was really there and not a vision.

I saw little drops of the blood dripping back up to heaven. I watched little specks dripping upward, and I saw that the blood was sparkling with heavenly light. It looked alive, and it was so pure that I knew one drop of this blood was more than enough to cleanse the whole universe. The teardrop itself was about five inches high, three inches wide, and had a halo surrounding it.

My eyes then examined the halo of light that surrounded the blood. I have never seen a light like this. It looked like millions of tiny dots of white light, and mixed in with these dots were millions of rainbow-colored dots that mingled together in absolute perfection. Everything was sparkling like diamonds, and the overall appearance was beautiful and glorious.

Before I could tell my friends about this, I heard Lynn exclaiming, "He is covered in the blood! I can see it! I can see it!" I got a good long look at this heavenly teardrop and was able to describe in detail what I was seeing. Before long it vanished and all I saw was the typical darkness when one's eyes are closed.

"Whew!" That's all I could say after that. We rejoiced at this unbelievable miracle. Why had God let me see the blood? I knew that Jesus had shed tears of blood before He went to the cross, but this experience still didn't make much sense to me. However, I realized that if it is written in the Word, then it is a fact whether we understand it or not. But what shocked me most was that this was no vision. The teardrop was really there. I could see that it had height and depth, and it was moving and seemed to be alive. How this can be still remains a mystery to me.

But what did it mean? I have found that God never does something "just because." He had a reason for letting me see this magnificent sight, and I was determined to find out what it was.

After I had lunch with Bill, it was time to head home to Tacoma. As I headed north I was upset at wondering what this all might mean. Why was God showing me all these things? I don't feel like a holy man. In fact, I feel pretty sad about the way I lived my life. "Why, God? Why are You doing this to me?"

As I drove, I was so deep in thought that the miles passed without notice. Then, as I was passing the town of Kelso, I began to feel the power of God moving through me. I was looking out my window at the clouds that were upwards of twenty thousand feet above me. Behind the clouds it looked as if the sun was beginning to sparkle. The cloud layer was like a thin blanket covering the sky, and I started to see the light shimmering the way sunlight does on water. This didn't make any sense. I had watched the sky my whole life, and never had I seen such a sight.

The sun behind the clouds seemed to be bouncing and moving in an erratic pattern. Suddenly, the sun then split into three round balls of different sizes and then moved into a half-moon arc. The larger ball was on top, with the medium-sized ball in the middle and the small one on the bottom.

I almost crashed my car as I heard the off-lane warning bumps rattling under my tires. I was full of wonder and began asking God what He was doing to me. I steered my car back in its lane and looked up to see that the sky looked normal as always.

Stunned by spiritual experiences like these, I kept asking God why He was allowing me to see these things. Deep in thought, I looked up to see the sun begin to move again. It started to sparkle, and then it split into three equally sized balls of light and moved into a perfect triangle formation. This was an open-eyed vision, and I felt as if I was looking through some supernatural glasses that revealed unseen things.

I looked to see if my car was still in the lane. When I looked back at the sky, all was normal. The rest of the drive continued without incident. I drove the rest of the way with my radio off and my heart crying out for an answer to what this all meant. God did say we would see signs in the heavens; I know this was one of those signs.

Arriving home in the late afternoon I called Nick to tell him about the miracles. He asked me if I had the energy to go to a Bible study that night. I couldn't pass up the opportunity to tell him my story in person, so I went. Nick was greatly encouraged at my testimony. Both of us came up with a lot of speculation on what it all meant, but not knowing the scope of God's plan for our lives made it impossible to say for sure.

We arrived early to the Bible study, and as we sat in the meeting room waiting for things to start, the Lord spoke to me about the events of the day. As I sat there in silence, I heard God's voice say, "My son, I am about to bring a divine visitation to the Pacific Northwest. Tell my people to prepare their hearts."

The next morning I went about my usual business. It was Sunday morning, and I skipped church because I was exhausted. I decided to get an "Auto Trader" magazine to see what kind of automobile bargains I could find. As I looked at the date on the magazine, I suddenly couldn't remember what day it was. I stood in the store for a moment and drew a blank. Frustrated, I went to the store clerk and asked him if this was the current magazine for the week. He was Korean and didn't understand what I was asking.

All of a sudden, a man appeared at my side. He excused himself and then began telling me that the dates were off because it was leap year. I repeated the words "leap year," and he said, "Yes, leap year. You know, the year that we get one extra day in the month of February." He then said, "Yesterday was February 29; otherwise it would be March 1."

As he said this, a wave of God's power went through me, leaving behind goose bumps from head to toe. The day before was "February or March," depending on whether or not it was leap year. I left with the words God had spoken long before ringing in my ears: "February or March."

Our God is an awesome God. I now know this is exactly what God said it was. It was a sign to me that He is going to visit this area with His divine power. To confirm this, the Lord has led me to many people who have seen similar visions concerning the Pacific Northwest. I know that someday soon He will make good on that promise.

Three months after seeing the magnificent angel at Bill's house, I noticed the Star of David symbol while attending a messianic Jewish church. It only took a few seconds before I realized that the symbols on the angel's chest and arms formed the Star of David.

Here is a graphic drawing depicting this truth.

DIAGRAM OF ANGEL SYMBOLS

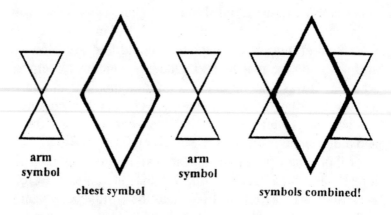

arm symbol   chest symbol   arm symbol   symbols combined!

One month after seeing the angel I noticed a flag bearing the "Star of David". I then realized the symbols on the angel's garment formed the same symbol when connected.

The graphic above demonstrates this fact and confirms that he was one of God's angels sent to protect me while I slept.

Signs, Wonders, and Miracles

A fter seeing the blood of Jesus, I was filled with awesome wonder. If God is going to pour out His divine power in this area, then something big is going to happen that the whole world is going to know about. This is the only conclusion that I can come up with that makes any sense. I have heard of miracles in parts of the world that should start world-impacting revivals, things like people being raised from the dead and visitations from Jesus.

If these types of things do not impact our world, then God must be planning something pretty big to get the world's attention. I feel He is going to do a number of things so miraculous that no one will be able to deny the supernatural origin of the events. Even so, multitudes will deny God and His deity. The Bible says that the hearts of the people will become so hardened by sin that they will deny God in the face of miracles.

With anticipation of God moving in our midst, I became more determined to draw close to Him for safety and direction. It was after seeing the teardrop that God began to show me vision after vision of endtime events. Every two weeks or so God would drop in on my dreams to give me a little more information that could later be used to warn the people.

At the same time, things began to happen in churches and Bible studies that God used to teach me about His supernatural nature.

With my heart set on fire for God, I began to visit as many Bible studies as I could fit into the week. Still unable to work, I was thankful to find a lot of opportunities to do just that. One night at Lynn's Bible study a miracle happened that taught me an important lesson.

I had arrived at 7 p.m. to find the house already full of people. I became excited, wondering what God had in store for us this night. I wanted to just sit and learn, so I decided I was going to sit quietly and keep my ears open and my mouth shut.

Just then, Bill asked me to pray for him. He had been through a lot. Four years earlier, a divorce had hurt him deeply. On top of that, he lost his job and only source of income, leaving him feeling shipwrecked. He then got the bad news that he now had diabetes and needed to go on medication. The diabetes test results had come in a week earlier, and he was devastated. Wondering why all this was happening to him, he was desperate to hear from God.

His desperation motivated him to seek prayer and not give up. He kept asking, and I kept on saying that I wasn't in the mood to pray. It isn't like me to turn down an opportunity to pray for my friends, but I was really feeling like a spectator that night and felt that it was a waste of time to pray with this mindset. After asking me five times, I agreed to pray for him before the night was over.

The night went by in a hurry, and finally it was time to pray for Bill. We seated him in the middle of the room, and I put my right hand on his left shoulder and began to pray. I was praying away and the people were intensely watching, hoping God would give me a word for Bill. After a few minutes in prayer they started asking me if I was getting anything. Frustrated, I shook my head no.

At that point I was ready to give up. I was sure God wouldn't speak to me in my unspiritual mindset. I remember thinking, *This is ridiculous, God. What am I doing praying for Bill anyway?* I heard God say, "My son, hold your left hand up, pray in the Spirit, and be ready to receive."

I did what God commanded. I lifted my left hand waist high, palm up, and began praying in the Spirit. Instantly, a Bible appeared in my left hand. Although it was a vision, I could see it clearly. The Bible was open and the pages were sparkling white, but they had no words on them. I was shocked to see how white the pages were, and I knew this book had a heavenly origin.

Just then God put a question in my mind. I heard my mind ask God this question, and yet I somehow knew that it was His mind I was thinking with: "God, You must have a scripture for Bill—what is it?"

Instantly, on the top of the right page, words formed. It looked as if an invisible hand came down and wrote these words while I watched: "Job Chapter 2." This writing was in the most beautiful calligraphy I had ever seen; I was shocked as I watched the words form before my eyes. At the same time, I heard these words: "Verse 1 through 7."

Then the Bible disappeared as suddenly as it had appeared. At the time I had no idea what was in the book of Job, let alone what was written in Job 2:1-7. Not wanting to say what I had just seen, I grabbed my Bible and found the book of Job.

Reading from the second chapter of Job, I was overwhelmed with joy. Job was in a similar situation to Bill, or should I say, Bill was in a similar spot as Job. The Book of Job starts out with Satan and God having a conversation before God's throne. God asks Satan if he had seen how great a man Job was and how he loved God with all his might.

Satan replied by telling God that Job loved Him because God had blessed him with all manner of blessing and had a protective hedge around him so Satan couldn't touch him. Satan then challenged God and said that if God let him destroy Job's life, Job would curse God to His face.

God then said that all of Job's possessions could be in Satan's hands, but Satan was told that he could not touch Job. Satan then took all of Job's wealth and killed all of Job's children. This Old Testament book recalls Job's mourning over his great loss and is a witness that Job still praised God and never turned his heart away from the Lord.

Job 2 opens with Satan coming again to God with a new challenge. This is the exact passage the Lord gave me for Bill: "Again there was a day when the sons of God came to present themselves before the Lord, and Satan came also among them to present himself before the Lord. And the Lord said unto Satan, From whence comest thou? And Satan answered the Lord, and said, From going to and fro in the earth, and from walking up and down in it. And the Lord said unto Satan, Hast thou considered my servant Job, that there is none like him in the earth, a perfect and an upright man, one that feareth God, and escheweth evil? and still he holdeth fast his integrity, although thou movest me against him without cause. And Satan answered the Lord, and said, Skin for skin, yea, all that a man hath will he give for his life. But put forth thine hand now, and touch his bone and his flesh, and he will curse thee to thy face. And the Lord said unto Satan, Behold, he is in thine hand; but save his life. So went Satan forth from the presence of the Lord, and smote Job with sore boils from the sole of his foot unto his crown" (Job 2:1-7).

This is precisely the situation Bill was in. First, he lost his family through divorce. Then, his means of making money was taken away. Bill held fast to his testimony through all these trials, and then, without warning, he came down with a physical ailment as Job did. This couldn't be any plainer, unless God Himself appeared and said, "Bill, you are going through a test to see if you will still serve Me when things go wrong."

This event greatly encouraged Bill and taught me an important lesson. I learned that praying in the Spirit is a powerful tool and should be exercised as often as possible. I also learned that God doesn't need us to be in a praying mood to visit us with His presence. It helps to be in a state of prayer all the time, but God can show up whenever He wants and reveal Himself to whomever He chooses. Thank You, dear God, for showing Yourself to Your undeserving servant—me.

Shortly after this, I was in Tacoma praying with some friends that met weekly for Bible reading and fellowship. The time had come to pray for individual needs, and someone asked me if I would pray for Sandy, who hosted the weekly meetings. Not feeling quite up to that by myself, I asked Nick if he would join me. Now Nick is a very shy person, and not wanting to have the attention focused on him, he asked Jose to join us as we gathered around Sandy to pray.

The next few moments were awkward as the three of us encircled Sandy, who was sitting in the middle of the room. None of us seemed to want to start. We just stood there in silence as the tension grew.

I began asking God silently if I should pray, and I kept getting the feeling to wait. I didn't have anything to pray at the moment, so I stood there waiting for someone to break the silence. Finally, Nick began to pray. He prayed a short prayer, and then it was back to silence.

That is when I became nervous. I was drawing a big blank, and Jose was keeping silent. God finally spoke to me and said to wait because Jose was about to pray. Now Jose is a big man, about six-foot-four and around three hundred pounds. He was originally from Mexico and speaks only broken English.

He immediately started praying in Spanish after God gave me the signal to wait. Jose was suddenly filled with the Spirit and began to pray as loud as I had ever heard someone pray. He was shaking all over, and with his eyes closed, he bobbed and moved and shook as he prayed for a good five minutes in Spanish. I didn't understand a single word he said, but I felt it was truly from God.

Suddenly, he quit praying, and the Holy Spirit let me know what to pray. I boldly prayed a very long prayer that covered quite a few subjects. I was filled with the Spirit and could feel the presence of the Lord as I poured out what God had given me to pray.

I prayed until I felt a release. After praying the words the Lord had given me, I heard someone sobbing behind me. I turned to see Jose's wife curled up in her chair, crying like a baby. She started saying something to her husband, but it was in Spanish, and I didn't understand what was being said.

When she had finished talking, Jose's eyes were filled with excitement. He then came up to me and said, "I must hug you, brother, I must hug you." His huge frame engulfed me with a bear hug that lasted quite a while.

After he let me go, I turned to his wife and asked her to please explain what was going on. Still crying, she told us that I prayed word for word what her husband had prayed in Spanish. We were all filled with joy and amazement as we began to thank God for His awesome presence.

I felt on top of the world. God was moving in my life, and I was filled with a joy that I had never known. I knew that despite our pitiful condition, the Spirit of the Lord can change an ordinary prayer into powerful, life-changing words that can break bondages, heal wounds, and change hearts.

Shortly after this, my good friend Bill moved from Beaverton Oregon to Seattle to take a job with a Christian publisher. Through the leading of the Lord, he met Len

Phelps, the pastor of Shiloh Fellowship of Mountlake Terrace. Bill started attending his church and began to see miraculous things taking place. Not having a home church of my own, I began to commute to Shiloh each Sunday. This turned out to be a blessing as God met us there each Sunday.

For the next few months I attended regularly, and each and every meeting was a bigger blessing than before. It turned out that the whole ministry team had been receiving visions from the Lord, just as I had. Len was amazed when we compared notes. God had been giving them the same messages over the years, and it moved us to see that the Lord was showing many others what was in store for the future of God's church.

Each Sunday I would look forward to praising our Lord and spending time in His presence. One Sunday service something happened that I will never forget. It started, as usual, with praises to God. The Bible says, "But thou art holy, O thou that inhabitest the praises of Israel" (Psalm 22:3). That day I found that God really does inhabit our praises.

As we were singing, the power of God surrounded me. I started shaking all over and felt God's powerful presence as I continued singing with all my might. At Shiloh, they praise God with all their heart. Sometimes Len forgoes preaching as God's Spirit takes over for His own purposes. This was going to be one of those times. As I sang with my eyes closed and my hands shaking from the power of God, I heard Len say in a loud voice, "Brother, the power of God is upon you to prophesy, so in Jesus' name, prophesy." Even though my eyes were closed, I knew these words were directed to me, because they came at me like an arrow and pierced my heart with power.

My left arm was raised up seemingly on its own power. It almost felt as if it was propelled in the air by some supernatural power. Suddenly I found myself in another place altogether. I was standing under a stone archway that was clearly in a place not on earth. My body seemed to be weightless, and I didn't need to breathe the whole time I was standing under this archway.

The archway was constructed of stone that was illuminated internally with the light of God. It looked like metal glowing in a hot furnace. I took a good look at this heavenly structure. It was about seven feet to the top of the arched ceiling, and about five feet separated the vertical walls. The entire inside surface was jagged, in a pattern that looked like it was made of triangles laid side by side. This archway seemed to engulf me with the warmth of eternal light.

Just then, words started floating down from heaven and directly into my mind. As I heard each word in my head, I heard my mouth speak it a second later. My mind seemed to be a third party that had nothing at all to do with this heavenly communication.

As these words went through me, I was filled with pure joy. Each word carried a feeling of pure love, and I heard my mind say the word "Wow" after each word spoken, because I was overwhelmed with pure love. This communication went on for some time. Three separate subjects were covered, and the main theme was the return of the Lord and the restoration of His authority to His prophets.

I was in the Spirit and oblivious to what was going on around me. When I finally came back to my earthly senses, I realized they had hooked me up to a wireless microphone and recorded what was spoken. The gist was that God is going to do a new thing in His people, and it is going to be glorious. The Bible puts it this way: "Behold, I will do a new thing; now it shall spring forth; shall ye not know it? I will even make a way in the wilderness, and rivers in the desert" (Isaiah 43:19).

Shortly after the archway miracle, I had another experience that was as baffling as it was beautiful. I was attending a Saturday meeting with Nick. We were entering into the praise and worship with all our hearts when the Lord spoke directly to me: "He who is forgiven much loves much, and he who is forgiven little loves little."

Suddenly I was out of my body and I found myself standing in a place that was clearly not of this earth. I could see myself standing in a square room that seemed to have been dug out of level ground. I was seeing this vision as if I was a third party looking down on myself. The walls went down about ten feet, and the room was shaped like a cube. I looked down the smooth walls to see myself waiting on the Lord. Perched above this unusual room, I saw what looked like a gold bench. But my eyes seemed to be focused down into this cubicle. I could see the bench out of the corner of my eye and remember thinking it could either be a throne or a bench.

Suddenly, a beautiful silver light shone down into the cubicle. It was as thick as smoke and yet as crisp as a laser beam. It looked like liquid silver as it shone down to illuminate this unusual cube. As the heavenly light filled the chamber, I watched myself standing at attention in the middle of the cube and waiting on God. At this point I began to dance in the silver light, and I could see that I was wearing a yarmulke on my head.

As I watched myself dancing in the light, I knew this particular dance had special meaning. I watched as my poetry-like motion offered up praise and thanksgiving to the Lord. I was completely filled with love for the Lord and was thanking Him for His mercy through this dance offering. At this point my whole being was taken captive by God's presence. Suddenly I was back in my body with my eyes closed and my head twirling around and around, spinning me gently out of this vision.

I was filled with emotion as I wiped the tears from my eyes. I needed to be forgiven much. I had done a lot of sinful things. I also knew that by God's grace was I able to enter into His body, the church. This has humbled me and filled me with thanksgiving for the forgiveness of my sins.

In the Bible, Jesus said this about a prostitute and her sinful condition: "Wherefore I say unto thee, her sins, which are many, are forgiven; for she loved much: but to whom little is forgiven, the same loveth little" (Luke 7:47). I was just like that prostitute in the respect that I had been forgiven much. I thank God that my sins will not be counted against me on the Day of Judgment. I now see that my heart has fallen in love with Jesus because of the abundant thanksgiving that comes when one is pardoned for sins that deserve the fullest measure of penalty—eternal death.

Looking back, I marveled at the "word for word prayer" that Jose prayed in Spanish. I also marveled at seeing the Bible appear in my hands while praying for Bill. All of these things are wonderful and faith building, but this last event was something altogether different. I knew I had visited Heaven in this vision but I was to find out later that I had been in a very special place called the most holy place. This is how the Lord revealed this truth to me.

In the summer of 2008 I was driving home from work one sunny day listening to a sermon on the Ark of the Covenant and the holy place of God. I was paying close attention to the description of the most holy place, as I had never heard a sermon on this subject. Apparently the most holy place is a perfect cube. The dimensions were 15 by 15 by 15 feet. God warned Moses to build the tabernacle according to the pattern given him, because this earthly tabernacle was a copy of the most holy place in heaven.

Hearing this, I realized that I had been caught up in heaven and was standing in the most holy place of the Most High God. I believe the gold I noticed out of the corner of my eye was the gold covering the true Ark of the Covenant. We were attending a messianic Jewish church that day, and I was caught away while we were praising and worshiping God. It wouldn't surprise me a bit to find that we had been singing the song about the Holy of Holies when I was suddenly taken away in the spirit.

Around this time, I needed some insurance for my car, so I decided to check with a friend of my younger brother, K.C., who brokered all types of insurance. I was on my way to his office when the Lord spoke: "My son, you are not going to talk about insurance, you are going to witness for me."

Hearing this, I became excited wondering what God had in store for us. When I arrived, Joe, my brother's friend, was busy with a customer so I had to wait a few minutes before I got his attention. As I waited I could feel the Lord stirring my spirit, and I reviewed what I might say when the time came.

Before I knew it, the customer left, and the two of us were alone in the office. We greeted one another, and after the usual small talk the conversation turned to business. Joe asked me what he could do for me; I originally intended to ask about car insurance but I knew the Lord had salvation waiting for this man, so I began telling him about the visions and dreams. I gave it everything I had and held nothing back.

Joe listened intently, and after sharing my dreams and visions, I wanted to lead him to salvation by sharing the gospel. Before doing so I asked Joe if he attended church or understood the way to eternal life with God. Joe said he was unsure and didn't understand the concepts of salvation and eternal life. He admitted that he had been searching for the truth about God, but in two years of going to different churches, he was confused and didn't understand the gospel.

That was an open door for me to give him the gospel with both barrels. I explained in detail how Jesus came to earth to die for our sins and how without Him we could not go to heaven no matter how good we think we are. He got excited and started saying, "I understand, I understand. For the first time I know what it all means." The Lord revealed the truth to Joe and opened his spiritual eyes.

Joe was excited but wasn't ready to make a commitment. He asked if he would feel anything supernatural happen if he received the Lord. I told him that when I received the Lord I just felt joy, but later I began to feel God's power as I drew close to Him.

Then Joe burst out, "OK, I'm ready, I'm ready." We held hands and prayed the sinner's prayer, in which we acknowledge our sins and ask Jesus to save us and be our Lord and Savior. As soon as we prayed, the Holy Spirit came pouring down from above. Both of us felt God's power moving.

Joe began to cry and said, "Now I am going to tell you a miracle." Something had happened to him the previous day that he hadn't intended to tell anyone about. The previous weekend he had taken his wife to Canada for a short break. As they walked along a beach, he received an open-eyed vision from God in which he noticed an unusual looking clamshell and picked it up to take a closer look. As he examined it in his hands, it opened up, and the light of God came flooding out from inside. The voice of God spoke to him in the light: "My son, you are having a hard time finding Me. Do not worry; I am sending My messenger to you."

He had that vision the day before I showed up to lead him to Jesus. I rejoiced, knowing that God will be found by those who seek after Him with all their heart and soul. He promised this in His Word through this scripture: "For every one that asketh receiveth; and he that seeketh findeth; and to him that knocketh it shall be opened" (Matthew 7:8).

Knowing this, I wonder why anyone would refuse the free gift of eternal life found only in Jesus Christ, the King of kings and the Lord of lords.

♦ 12 ♦

God Commands — Write a Book

The Bible says God is the Giver of all good things. I have learned this truth as I have made my way through life. I have also learned that God gives us His gifts for a reason. If He gives you the gift to prophecy, it is to be used to help His body, the church. If your gift is generosity, then God wants you to give liberally to whomever he puts in your path who has a need.

In my case, God had given me a treasure in the different dreams and visions. What I was starting to sense was that He wanted me to share my visions with anyone and everyone who would listen. I was building quite a big inventory of information and was ready to tell the world, if the world would only listen.

I knew God wanted me to write a book about these messages from above but wondered who would listen to an unemployed middle-aged man with no formal Bible training. I pushed the thought aside while I continued receiving more and more visions from the Lord.

I began feeling restless. I had not worked for two years, and each day that I came out to the kitchen to greet my folks became harder than the last. I was still depressed and the thought of returning to sales was out of the question. I knew

I couldn't take that kind of pressure, but not having any other skills, I didn't know where to turn.

Wanting to serve God and Him alone, I began praying for something to do that had eternal meaning. One morning I got up before my parents to get away and think. I was at Denny's having coffee when the waitress showed me a special cup that bore an image that went from a frowning face when it was cold to a smiling face after hot coffee was poured in.

I got the idea to make cups that preach the gospel using this technique. It took only two months to find the right sources and get the first cup made. This first and best cup was a dramatic scene with Jesus hanging on the cross with black clouds above. When hot liquid is poured in, the scene changes to a beautiful rainbow above an empty cross with the words "He Has Risen" written in the rainbow.

Marketing this cup was a lot of fun. I started with one design and ended up with seven. This took up the slack in my life and made home life much easier, as we enjoyed the process of watching each new design develop from a little idea to the finished product.

I enjoyed designing the cups but had no way to get them out to the public. It just so happened that a man in Portland had been thinking about selling our T-shirts a few years back. He had changed his mind but told me to look him up if I ever came up with a new product.

I contacted him about the cups, and after he looked at my designs, we signed a seven-year contract, giving him the job of marketing God's cup. This was God's way of taking care of me when I was too sick to work. Each month I would get a check in the mail, and all I had to do was work on getting healed and serving God.

I could see how the Lord had already prepared for me being in trouble. He used the T-shirt excursion to get me in touch with the man who would later market my gospel cups. For the next year or so I followed the Lord and attended as many Bible studies and meetings as I could find. I began to realize I was ready for some new challenges.

The fourth and final year that I lived with my parents became a year of transition. The Lord was going to set His plans in motion, but first He had to get me thinking in the right direction. Nick and I did a lot of fasting and praying back then, and God was speaking to my heart more than ever. I knew He wanted me to write a book about the miracles. He had shown me this time and time again.

What I lacked was the faith to believe I could actually write a book that anyone would care to read. Back then I was still healing and didn't think I could take on that kind of project. Knowing my lack of conviction, God was about to show me beyond a doubt that His plan for me was to write a book about Him.

At about this time, many of my Christian friends were questioning the dreams I had been receiving. I couldn't really blame them, because these things are hard to understand and rarely discussed. Many of the visions God had given me personally had already come to pass, but the visions concerning the world were still on the horizon.

I became frustrated with the situation and prayed for further confirmation that I was on track. God, being the compassionate friend He is, answered my prayers almost immediately. One night I was fed up with myself for not going out and telling the world what God had shown me. I knew the dreams were important; there was no question about that. What I didn't have was a clear picture on how to go about proclaiming God's message. I thought about preaching it in the streets but felt I wasn't ready for that kind of ministry work. Then I thought about Christian television but felt the Lord had other avenues to get the message out. Not knowing which way to turn, I did what most Christians do when they need guidance—I prayed.

I started praying with all my heart for God to show me what to do. I needed to know, and I needed to know right now. One night as I was praying for direction, I heard God's voice telling me to get my Bible and open it up so He could show me His perfect will.

I grabbed my Bible and said a quick prayer, thanking Him for showing me what to do. Then I closed my eyes, opened up my Bible, and I placed my finger on the spot that I felt God wanted me to see. I then opened my eyes and began to read the scripture I was pointing to. (This may sound like a foolish thing to do, but let me tell you that many times God has spoken to me in just this fashion.) If the God who created the universe can't open a book to a certain page, He can't be much of a God. God can do anything, and I'm constantly filled with joy when He does what seems impossible.

This is the Scripture that lay directly under my finger: "I will stand upon my watch, and set me upon the tower, and will watch to see what he will say unto me, and what I shall answer when I am reproved. And the Lord answered me, and said, Write the vision, and make it plain upon tables, that he may run that readeth it. For the vision is yet for an appointed time, but at the end it shall speak, and not lie: though it tarry, wait for it; because it will surely come, it will not tarry" (Habakkuk 2:13).

Reading this scripture made my hair stand on end. This confirmed God's plan for me to write a book. I found out three days later that He was going to keep confirming this plan until I finally wrote my first word years later. After receiving this confirming scripture, I began asking God what to name this book of dreams and visions. I had an idea of how I wanted the cover to look but the actual name eluded me. Each day I would pray and ask God what to name the book as I went about my daily routine.

I had been praying for three days, asking God to give me an answer. I had just received a shipment of my "He

Has Risen" coffee cups and went over to Mama Johnson's to show off my new cup. Mama was a Spirit-filled grandma who loved the Lord with all her might. She and I were close friends before the Lord took her home. We prayed together often. I was so excited that day, and I couldn't wait to see her eyes sparkle when she saw my new cup in action.

When I arrived at her place, we talked about the Lord for a while, and then I pulled out my new cup for her to see. She liked it very much but didn't know that it was going to change when she poured coffee into it. (I left that as a surprise.)

When she poured the coffee, her eyes suddenly opened wide with surprise. She watched as Jesus disappeared off the cross and the black cloud vanished. Then God spoke to me the second time about writing my book. When Mama saw the rainbow over the cross and read the words "He Has Risen" written in the rainbow, she looked up and said, "That's what you are supposed to name your book."

Instantly I responded, "Who told you I was writing a book?" With that she thought for a second and then belted out a "Glory, hallelujah!" She said those words came out of her mouth before she had time to think. We knew this was a message from God and I told her the whole story right from the beginning.

After this, "I knew that I knew" what God wanted me to do. I began to visualize how I would write my book and what I might say. I also began to verbalize my plans for writing this book to my friends. It's kind of funny how some people think. You can know them pretty well and think they respect you, only to find that in a pinch they turn their backs and look the other way. I found this to be true of some of my so-called friends when it came to the subject of this soon-to-be-written book.

One so-called friend came against me by ridiculing the dreams I had shared with her. This turned out for God's glory, because the Lord Himself defended my honor in a supernatural way. This made a believer out of her and gave me another confirmation to push ahead.

During a home fellowship meeting, I had shared some of the things the Lord had shown me. This particular friend seemed upset at some of the visions of judgment I shared and told me that God wanted to bless this world, not destroy it. Not wanting to get into a conversation that would disrupt the meeting, we dropped the subject and continued on.

A week later she called saying she needed to talk to me that minute. I said goodbye to the other person on the line and got back to her to find out what could be so urgent. She started by apologizing for treating me the way she did at the Bible study. She admitted being afraid of the thoughts of disaster in our world and got upset when I brought up the subject. She then told me her real reason she was calling.

She told me that in prayer she began to tell God what a big dreamer I was. Not wanting the things that I shared to be true, she then told God that the dreams I had shared were fake. Just after she had said this to the Lord, He replied audibly, saying, "Joseph was a dreamer, and it was I who gave him the dreams." She recounted hearing God's voice out loud, just as we speak in our daily conversation, but He said these words forcefully, as if pressing His point. Startled, she asked, "Lord, what are You going to do?" The Lord responded, "You just wait and see."

After hearing her testimony I was filled with joy. I want everyone to accept the visions and dreams as genuine, and it hurts when they don't. In this last confirmation, God was showing me a couple of things. First and foremost, the dreams and visions are valid. I already knew this, but I thank God each time He confirms this, and I look forward to the next time God reaches down from heaven to encourage my progress. Secondly, the majority of people are going to reject my testimony. I have this feeling that I'm going to come under much criticism over this book. In the Bible, virtually all of God's servants went through this type of persecution. Knowing this, "I press toward the mark for the prize of the high calling of God in Christ Jesus" (Philippians 3:14).

Shortly after this last confirmation God reconfirmed to me the validity of the visions and His call on my life. This one event proved without question that I had been hearing from God and provided the unshakable evidence I needed to drive me forward in the face of opposition and resistance from people.

During a period of intense fasting and prayer, the Lord brought a wave of visions that set my heart and spirit on fire. Wanting to spend all my time with people who love God, I began to meet with Nick as often as our schedules would allow. We would spend our time reading God's Word and discussing His awesome works. Our favorite place to meet was a Denny's restaurant not far from where we both lived.

One day while we were discussing the Lord, a waitress came up to us with a look of shock on her face. She said she had overheard us talking about the miracles God had done in our lives, and she wanted to hear more. She asked us if we would consider meeting her and a friend after work to tell them about the times we saw Jesus and describe some of the dreams the Lord had given us. We agreed to meet the following Thursday and went back to our meal and conversation.

The following Wednesday I got a call from Nick. He had to work the next day and was unable to get the time off for our meeting. I was unemployed at the time and wanting to serve the Lord in any capacity, so I decided to go by myself to testify about the miracles that God had let me see.

Thursday finally came, and before I knew it I was sitting across the table from these two women telling them about the dreams, visions, and moves of God that I had been an eyewitness to. They were greatly encouraged and shared some of their own testimonies.

The waitress we originally met was working at Denny's to finance a Christian album she was producing. Her friend was a missionary who had traveled the world serving the Lord in many countries. She said she didn't believe my testimony, didn't like me, and felt I was either crazy or a modern-day Moses.

Both women said they were long-time Christians, and neither had met anyone with a testimony like mine. I understood their skepticism, because at times even I wondered if I was crazy myself.

Knowing my testimony was true I told them to ask God and told them He would reveal the truth about my testimony. We all agreed on this wisdom and finished drinking our coffee.

After saying everything that could be said, our meeting ended, and we all headed in different directions. As I drove away I thanked God for the opportunity to give my testimony and wondered if my message would take root in their hearts. I knew God had arranged this meeting, so I had faith that something good would come of it.

Four months would pass before I would visit my favorite restaurant again. I had been on a forty-day fast with Nick. We ate only fruits and vegetables as we denied our physical bodies to strengthen our spiritual lives. Just before the fast ended, the Lord told me that the final three days of our fast were going to be special. Excited at what God might do, I looked forward to the end of our fast.

Time seemed to drag from this point on but the moment of truth finally came. We made it through, and the final three days of our fast were suddenly upon us. The first of the three days happened to be a Saturday. I rose early that day in anticipation of God keeping His promise.

I started the day out with a simple prayer asking God to keep His promise and do mighty things in our lives. Immediately after praying this prayer God spoke to my heart. I did not hear His voice out loud, but I clearly heard His voice inside telling me to go to Denny's. Can you imagine that? The God who created the heavens and the earth was telling me to go to Denny's. It sounds too bizarre to believe, but nevertheless it is true.

After that God put it on my heart to visit Steve Johnson and then Fred and Pearl Penning to tell them about the miracles that God was doing in my life. Wanting to obey God in all things, I got dressed and headed out with much anticipation, wondering what the Lord had planned for me that day.

Before I knew it I was standing in the lobby at Denny's waiting for a table to open up. I have to admit that I began to wonder what was going on. I had a hard time believing that anything supernatural could happen over a cup of coffee, but I knew God had spoken to me and I was excited to think that God is able to do anything, anytime, anywhere.

As I stood wondering about these things, someone startled me by calling my name. I looked in the direction of the voice to see the waitress I had witnessed to four months prior. She happened to be working that morning and was glad to see me standing in the lobby.

We chatted for a minute, and I told her about my fast and the fact that God had sent me there for some unknown reason. She got really excited and told me that the friend that I had witnessed to four months prior was on her way down for a cup of coffee. She asked me if I would stick around to share more testimonies with them.

I began to sense that God had something in mind, so I accepted the invitation with anticipation and excitement. Looking around I noticed that the place was packed, so I decided to wait in the lobby for a booth to open up. As I waited, I began to feel the power of God rising up in my spirit. I turned around to look out the glass door and I saw the girl I had witnessed to four months earlier coming around the corner.

She was walking with her head down as if in a big hurry, and she looked up to find me directly in her path. It took her a second or two to realize who I was, and then she just lost it.

She started yelling out, "It's a miracle! It's a miracle!" Her eyes were wild, and she was shaking as if she had seen a ghost. I watched as her eyes filled with tears, and she kept shaking all over and saying things like "I can't believe it! It's a miracle! It's a miracle!"

I started asking her what was going on and thought I was missing something earthshaking right in my midst. She tried to regain her composure to answer, but it took a couple of tries before she could convey her thoughts in a rational, understandable way.

She said she had met ministers from all over the world but never had she heard things like I had shared with her four months earlier. She said my testimony upset her, because she didn't understand why the Lord would show so many things to a man who had little Bible education.

Then she said that my testimony had stayed in her mind to the point where it was almost plaguing her. That very morning she woke up with my testimony burning in her heart. She said it bothered her so much that she got down on her knees and put my testimony to the test. She said in prayer, "God, if this testimony is real, if that man is a true man of God sent by You, then as a sign to me, he will be standing in the lobby of Denny's when I arrive this morning."

Well, I don't have to tell you that I was more than encouraged. We had "church" right there in the restaurant. It was truly a blessed meeting. As we discussed the major topics of my dreams and visions, both women got so excited that they jumped up at the same time and started yelling, "What are you doing in Tacoma? Get out and proclaim God's message to the world!"

The rest of the day went much the same, and by the end of the weekend I had enough confirmation to write ten books. God had done exactly what He said He was going to do, and now I was more than determined to do my part and write God's book no matter what the cost.

I began to set my mind on how I was going to take on this major task. First, I needed to get healed so I could think well enough to write, and then I'd need a computer. After that I'd need to learn how to use the computer, and then I'd need...so much more.

♦ 13 ♦

Set Free for Service

Jesus said to His disciple Peter, "Watch and pray, that ye enter not into temptation: The spirit indeed is willing, but the flesh is weak" (Matthew 26:41). This is a fact that one cannot deny. Having been a Christian for quite some time, I have had many opportunities to see just how weak my flesh really is by falling many times in my daily walk with God.

What I have learned, however, is that our loving God accepts us just as we are. Then He fills us with His Holy Spirit and helps us to become what we are going to be. In between, there is the wilderness experience where God uses fiery trials to remove bad habits and unwanted character flaws from our lives.

This process is rather painful but the end results are well worth it. After this cleansing, we come out like gold refined in the fire, set free and ready to follow God wherever He may lead. The Bible equates this process to refining metal by fire. Only in the fiery furnace can the "dross" or impurities be removed from the metal. Most people resist this cleansing because it is so painful. Some preachers actually preach that bad times are a sign that a person has no faith or has hidden sin in their life. By preaching these things they have put a lot of good people in spiritual bondage by laying a yoke of guilt on them. What they deliberately forget is that the Bible clearly states: "Many are the afflictions of the righteous, but the Lord delivereth him out of them all" (Psalm 34:19).

The word *affliction* means "pressures." These pressures come in various forms. Whatever the pressure may be, you can be sure that God is allowing these things in your life to bring about positive changes in you for His glory.

In my case I had a lot of changing to do, so naturally I had a lot of afflictions to endure. I've described a few of the trials that God allowed in my life; I could actually write another book about the things I learned through these trials. Looking back, I can see how God molded me into a new person through this suffering. I now thank God for the trials, but I can honestly say that I am thrilled to leave those hard days behind.

The Bible says we endure hardship for a season and then comes the victory. In my case I had stood the test and had not given up my testimony for Jesus. The Lord let me know in many ways that it was now time to stand up and get into the battle. I knew exactly what God wanted me to do. You would think all I had to do was grab a pen and start writing.

In my case it was a little more complicated than that. I was still weak from the years of suffering. I kept trying to restart my life only to end up back in that old bedroom crying my eyes out. I was afraid to move ahead because I was not quite sure how to move or where to start.

God knew exactly what I needed and where He wanted me to go, and He was about to give me a helping hand out of my frustrating situation. He showed me His intention to help by giving me another dream that was a peek into the not-too-distant future.

I went to sleep one night perplexed at my lack of motivation and direction. I kept on trying to pick a path, but I just couldn't seem to get a vision that I felt was worthy of God's calling. One night I found myself in another dream walking on that highway made of water. I looked down to see that my feet were skipping along the surface of the water just as if it was pavement. Not surprised at this (I had seen this before), I looked up to see that I was coming to a spot in the highway that arched up like a bridge. It was quite steep, and each time I tried to get up the grade I would slide back down. I tried and tried to get up to the top, only to slide back to the bottom of the hill. I knew this represented my efforts to start living a new life. Tired of my repeated attempts to get up the hill, I was about to give up my efforts.

Suddenly, out of nowhere, a woman appeared at my right side. She was standing about an arm's reach away. She looked about 50 years old and had kind eyes that seemed to see deep into my heart where my emotions were hiding. As I turned to look into her face, she asked me this simple question, "Scott, why haven't you gone up?" I responded, "I can't; it's too steep, and I keep sliding back." She then said, "I will go with you, and together we will make it."

She then reached out her right index finger and touched the top of my right hand. Instantly, we were at the top of the hill. She disappeared before I could say a word, and then a woman came up to my right side and took my hand. We started walking down the straight and narrow highway as I watched from behind. We were heading straight for the eastern horizon, and the sun was just rising to light our path.

I knew God was going to help me get to the top. He was going to help me in my walk with Him, and I was going to make it. I also felt He was saying that He had a helpmate for me, someone I had yet to meet. I felt this was a picture of a future partner who would walk by my side and share in the joy of service to God.

Shortly after this, I had two more dreams that confirmed God had this partner for me. I was excited about the possibilities, but there were a few problems that had to be solved before this could happen. First of all, I was still unemployed, and this is not too conducive for attracting a wife. Also, I still needed deliverance from my emotional wounds that had led me to use alcohol as a painkiller and an emotional escape.

Knowing it was time to get going created a lot of pressure internally. I knew I needed to clean up my drinking habit and that it was not going to be easy. I had come out of a world so filled with pain that I know I would not have stood up under the pressure without some form of relief. I had become more dependent on this substance than I cared to admit, and I was not yet ready to let it go and get healed.

Knowing this, God gave me a little push in the right direction and got me to change my attitude about this problem. One night after a late-night Bible study, I returned home with a huge headache. I used to get these headaches often, because I had a hard time relaxing around people in my broken condition. Arriving home, I decided to have a glass of wine to help my headache and relieve the tension in my shoulders. I sat at the kitchen table and pondered the night's events. It had been a great night of prayer, and I was excited about the move of the Lord. Wanting to review some scripture before I went to sleep, I got my Bible and sat down to read.

Just before I opened my Bible, the thought came to me to make a whiskey and Coke instead of the wine. I felt this was a good idea, because I was really tense and thought this would help me relax quicker. I got up, poured the drink, and sat down again to read the Word. The glass of wine was still sitting there. I thought, "If only the church could see me now; what a pathetic testimony after all God has done for me." I prayed and asked God to help me with my alcohol problem and then flipped my Bible open to see what random scripture I might discover.

As I looked down on the page, my eyes were drawn to a particular spot on the page. To my utter amazement these are the words I read: "But they also have erred through wine, and through strong drink are out of the way; the priest and the prophet have erred through strong drink, they are swallowed up of wine, they are out of the way through strong drink; they err in vision, they stumble in judgment" (Isaiah 28:7). I was looking at my glass of wine and my mixed drink while I read this warning, and I became filled with awe and fear. I did not want to err in vision, and I did not want to get off the right path through my foolish sin.

I wrote on the top of that page, "Beware." At that moment, I decided to get this problem out of my life. I began to cry out to the Lord for healing and deliverance. I knew I had to quit. I had been in denial all my life, and God was now dealing with this problem. This struggle went on for the next few weeks, and then one night God delivered me out of my bondage.

I was totally broken over some serious issues I had been dealing with. Being weak in flesh, I turned to my old ways of dealing with my emotions. I remember getting totally drunk that night, and quite frankly, I was miserable. I did not want to drink, I knew it was wrong, and yet I seemed unable to stop.

I went to bed full of sorrow. I actually stood in the middle of my room and cried for what seemed to be a good half-hour. I started to cry out to the Lord, "God, help me, God, help me!" Suddenly I heard the Lord speak audibly: "My kingdom is not of eating or drinking." I burst out crying, because I had been in bondage over this issue and thought God was going to cut me off any minute if I didn't repent. I went to sleep that night knowing God was not mad at me and that He was going to help me out of this mess.

The next morning I woke up to find the Lord urging me to open my Bible. It was no ordinary compulsion, and I knew it was God's Spirit urging me to get the Word and be ready to receive. I flew out of bed and got my Bible. I prayed and asked God to show me what He wanted me to see. Then I closed my eyes and opened my Bible. I had a sense of expectancy as I opened my eyes to see what was on the page. I looked down to read these words: "For the kingdom of God is not eating and drinking, but righteousness and peace and joy in the Holy Spirit" (Romans 14:17). Wow, what a great God we have!

I have learned that what we put into our mouths is not what makes us unclean. The Bible says that what comes out of our mouths is what defiles a person. I know beautiful people who love God yet have weak areas that plague them. But I see God always loving these people and in the end healing them. I have also learned that hating our brothers and having prideful hearts are far worse sins than drinking alcohol. If some hidden weakness like this is keeping you out of the kingdom of God, remember this: Jesus will enter any house where He is welcome. He said it this way, "All that the Father giveth me shall come to me; and him that cometh to Me I will in no wise cast out" (John 6:37).

I would like to plead with you this very minute. If you haven't received eternal life and forgiveness for your sins by receiving Jesus as your Lord and Savior, do it now. Come to Jesus while you still have a chance. Many of us do not even have a tomorrow to decide. I don't care what you have done in your past, Jesus is able to forgive you of anything.

Waking to this scripture drove home the point that I was still in God's grace. The unconditional love God has for me changed my heart on this subject. I was now compelled to quit drinking, to show God that I loved Him in return. This beautiful God loves us so much that He sent Jesus to die for our sins. I knew that the only way to give thanks to God was by living a good life and following His directives to the best of my abilities. I was determined to do just that and was ready to follow Jesus no matter what the cost.

Knowing that I was ready to give up this foolish habit, God was going to send me help from above. One night I woke to find myself laying face down on my stomach. I normally sleep on my back, so without thinking, I began to roll over to go back to sleep. As I was rolling over, the Lord spoke to me audibly, saying, "The just shall live by faith." I was so depressed I rolled over and said, "I am too tired, and I don't know how to do that." God responded by proclaiming, "See how I love my children—see how I help my children." I heard these words in about the same amount of time it took to roll over.

As my head hit the pillow, I had an open-eyed vision. I saw myself wandering in circles. As I tried to straighten out, I would veer off again in a new zigzag path that led nowhere. I watched and beheld the entire body of Christ wandering around in the same crazy path. It was the church, the body of Christ, and they were all going astray. Then something wonderful happened. A blast of warm air blew on us from above. This wind was quite powerful and spun us around like toy tops. When we stopped spinning I realized that we were all lined up in single file. Everyone was in order, and I knew God had healed me. I raised my arms high in the air and yelled with a loud voice, "God, You have healed me, even from alcohol!" With that I came out of this vision and thanked God for His healing power.

The next morning I awoke with hope in my heart. I wanted to get right, and now I knew God was going to help me. As I got out of bed to dress and the Lord spoke to me a second time. This time I heard His voice in my head: "It's not over until you say it's over." Immediately I knew what God meant. It was my decision. If I wanted healing I would have to make my stand.

With all the determination in the world, I said out loud, "God, I want to be healed. From this day forward I would rather die than drink alcohol." With that said, I felt the desire for alcohol lift off of me. Suddenly I felt clean and different. I was healed right there on the spot, in the privacy of my little bedroom. What a great and wonderful God; what a beautiful Savior we have in Jesus; and what a great lesson to learn! We must give it up and turn our backs on our sins to be healed. Because God won't violate our free will, it's not over until we say it's over.

I was healed from that day forward. Before, I wanted to drink every day and would yield to that desire only to regret I had ever tried it in the first place. Now I was free from that constant nagging desire that invaded my thoughts daily. Thank You, Jesus, for healing me.

Set free from this bondage, I was now ready to come into the presence of the Lord with none of the guilt that I had been so used to in the past. I must admit that I have turned to my old ways in moments of weakness and extreme stress. I am not too happy to admit this, but I am glad to report that although I have slipped, I am still free from that horrible feeling of dependency that I was so used to. I thank God that He has given me back my freedom, and I am going to use that freedom to serve Him alone.

With the healing process in motion, things began to change rapidly. I started working for the first time in four years. The Lord arranged a job for me working for a guy named Scott. He is good friend and a brother in the Lord. He owned a machine shop in a little town called Orting, which sits at the base of Mount Rainier. It is a quaint little town, and working for him proved to be rewarding both physically and spiritually.

Almost immediately my health started to return. Scott recalls watching this process and equated my healing to being shot out of a cannon. In no time flat I was up and running as if the last four years had been as normal as ever. Scott wanted to go into business with me to market my coffee cups, so we rented part of the building his machine shop was in and got started. We gave it a good show and after spending a lot of time and money with little results, we decided the Lord had other plans for that space. By God's leading we dedicated our building to God and set it up to have Christian meetings. We prayed and asked the Lord what to do next, and He gave us the idea to invite Shiloh fellowship to come and hold meetings in our building.

By God's leading, the ministry team of Shiloh moved from Seattle to the small town of Republic, located in the northeast part of our state. We felt they were the ones chosen for the task, and we called them to see if they could come and minister in our building. We found out they had already been prompted by the Lord to come back to this area and hold meetings. We were also blessed to find out they were planning on calling us to see if we could find them a place to minister. They were going to call us that very day, in fact, and we were all greatly encouraged to know God had it all under His wonderful control.

With our minds set on getting the meetings started, we borrowed fifty folding chairs and a portable pulpit from Shiloh. We fixed the building up and then set a date for the first meeting. Preparing for this first meeting became the driving force of my life, and the joy of the Lord was my constant companion as we forged ahead for God. I was about to find out that God was going to further heal me through this endeavor, and He also had a big surprise waiting for me in the very first meeting. These blessings were eventually going to lead to the fulfillment of God's promises to me and would also lead to my writing this book.

It was now December 1994, a week before our first meeting, and most of the preparations were complete. All we had to do was pray, fast, and call everyone we knew and invite them to attend. Little did I know as I was making the calls that God was setting things up to bless me in a most special way.

As I looked in my directory I noticed a phone number that I had called only three times in my life. It belonged to a young woman a friend had introduced me to a year earlier, hoping we might hit it off. I was hoping the same thing, because she was a beautiful lady, full of the Spirit of the Lord on the inside, and on the outside she was as pretty as a flower, with beautiful blonde hair and a heartwarming smile.

I called her a few times when we first met, but I could tell she was not in a place where she was open to new friends in her life, so I quit calling. Seeing her number, I decided to take a chance and invite her to the meeting. She picked the phone up after one ring and was surprised to hear my voice. I was surprised to find that she was still living in the area, because she mentioned she might be moving back to Eastern Washington.

I found out she was going through much of the same trials that I had just come through. She had become a Christian four years before, and right away her husband of six years became hostile to her new lifestyle and began to persecute her for her faith. She recalled doing everything she knew to keep her marriage together, but after two years of turmoil, her husband announced that he was leaving her. This left her broken and confused, with three young children to take care of and little support from her family and friends.

Through all this, the Lord was faithful to keep her little family safe and sound as they prayed daily for God to help them find peace in a troubled world. Knowing that God was faithful and desired to give them life more abundantly, they started praying for a godly man to come and be the missing link in their family.

Almost immediately God started to confirm that He had a man picked out to fill the position. He started speaking to her in many different ways to confirm this fact and had also been speaking to her about endtime issues. Through all these things her heart had been set on fire for Jesus. Wanting to hear all that the Lord was saying to the church, she accepted the invitation to attend our first meeting.

Seeing her for the first time in a year was interesting, and we immediately hit it off. As you probably have guessed, we fell in love, and a few short months later we got married. This marriage gave me the foundation and structure I needed to keep focused and do God's will. It changed the course of my life, and out of our union came two wonderful and beautiful children that I love with all my heart. The marriage didn't end well, for reasons I can't write about, but it was all-important in setting the stage for the next phase of God's plan for my life.

About a year after we married, the Lord started urging me to get into my calling by writing this book. I felt the Spirit of the Lord calling and knew it was time to step out in faith. I was not only feeling the Lord's prompting, but also all my Christian friends were encouraging me to get busy. My boss and friend Scott was constantly urging me to start my project, and that helped me to keep focused.

Scott has a singing ministry and loves the Lord with all his heart. He is a big man, six-foot-two, 250 pounds, and yet he has a gentle voice that reaches right down to the center of your heart. God has given him a world-class voice, and he is a prophetic psalmist. He was instrumental in my decision to move ahead with my project.

I started gathering my thoughts about the structure and content of God's book. I sat down one evening and cataloged all my dreams and visions and took a good look at all the information I had. I was truly overwhelmed as I counted over a hundred visions and dreams that I had received over the years. I soon realized that putting them in a book that could be understood was not going to be easy. It was a daunting task, but I had a sense of peace and knew the Lord would guide me through to completion.

I had a pretty good outline in my head as to the structure of my book. I was simply going to tell the story as it happened. This would be easy to do. I remember all the visions as if they happened yesterday, so all I had to do was start writing.

That was when I realized I lacked one thing to complete my project: a computer. Not only that, I had never used one before. I needed to purchase a computer, and I would need someone to teach me how to use it. Knowing this, the Lord brought a man named Bob into my life to help me. Bob is married to a wonderful and godly woman named Margaret.

Bob and Margaret lived across the street from my wife, Jenny, before we married. They invited us over for coffee, and we became instant friends. They are Spirit-filled Christians and serve the Lord with all their heart. Bob had years of computer experience and had done the layout of several Christian books and publications, including some things he wrote himself. He was a great help in proofing, editing, and working on the final layout of this book. Without his help, I may not have finished this project.

He helped me pick a computer for ease of use, a Macintosh, and gave me the additional hardware and software needed to do the job. He also taught me how to use it and helped me whenever I had a problem. With his computer skills he helped me edit the book and made it all work. All in all I am in great debt to Bob for all his help, and I know that God will reward his family for all the help and encouragement they have given me to see this project to completion.

With everything in place, it was apparent the moment of truth had come. It was time to start writing, and I had everything going for me. I was feeling good and working hard. I had the right equipment to write my book, and I had the encouragement and support I needed to push me ahead. I had all of these things, and yet I seemed to be stuck. I was now faced with one last hurdle that seemed to be unmovable:

I realized I didn't have enough stamina or hours in my day to write a book.

I would come home from work so tired that all I wanted to do was take a shower and go to bed. With a family of six, my day was just starting as I returned home to help my wife run our household and lead our family. A month went by, and I had only typed one page. It seemed hopeless. I realized that unless God changed things, I would never finish.

We began to pray for God to make enough time for me to get the job done. Shortly after that I was laid off due to a "temporary slump in business." This slump came in the midst of a booming economy that was fueled by the recent successes of the Boeing Company. My boss told me he needed to lay one of the workers off and wanted some advice in selecting the person. I immediately volunteered and knew this was God's answer to my prayers. I needed the time off to write my book, and this was it.

Having volunteered to take a break from work, I finished my last day on the job and went home praising the Lord. With nothing left to hinder me, I wrote my opening paragraph on May 11, 1996. It took three months to write. I worked on the book as if my life depended on it. With God's help I worked from morning to night as I was compelled to sit at the computer writing until I felt the Spirit withdraw. Time seemed to fly as I poured out my life's story. I was so full of joy, and I was totally focused on the goal. I have a hard time focusing due to chronic depression, so this was truly a miracle.

At the start of the project all went well, but finishing the book was harder than I expected. The enemy didn't like what I was doing and started attacking us daily. Each night we would go to sleep only to wake in the middle of the night and find that we were not alone in our comfortable little home. We were being visited by beings from the dark side. The Bible tells us that we wrestle not against flesh and blood but against principalities and powers and rulers controlled by our enemy, which is Satan.

We were being attacked spiritually. These attacks came in many forms and included the bed shaking so hard it would wake us up in fear. We would see shadows moving in the light, while having a feeling of total dread and fear. Both of us were having horrible dreams so demented that words can't describe the horror associated with them. My wife was terrified, and she had a hard time understanding it all. I had been through this type of terror many times in the past, and I was used to these kinds of attacks, but it was never easy.

But I kept faithful and focused on the book. We had so many attacks that I could write a book just on these events. At the same time God's Spirit was our companion, and the Lord gave us the power and desire to press on. God sent angels to guard our little home, and He allowed our young children to see them many times.

One night my wife's son came into the kitchen and told us he had seen a red flying saucer appear in his bedroom. He said it was about a foot in diameter, and it went into the closet and disappeared. I asked him what he thought it was, and he said the angel on the roof of our house told him it was a marker.

We were surprised at his reply. He told us there was a huge angel on the roof with a flaming sword in his hand. This was shocking and a bit hard to imagine, but I have seen angels, so I asked if he could talk to the angel and get his name.

He looked up towards the ceiling and immediately said, "His name is Gabriel." He spoke to this angel mind to mind because he didn't have time to ask the question out loud. This was surprising and exciting. He also said Gabriel told him the enemy had marked our home for an attack, and he was going to stand guard. He said he was going to call on another angel, Michael, if he needed him to fight the enemy.

I prompted him to ask Gabriel a few questions that I knew a young boy of 5 could not answer. Each time I asked a question I received an immediate and correct answer. This was most exciting, and we were full of awe knowing God's powerful angels were protecting us. This sort of thing kept happening over the three months it took to complete the book. All in all it was truly an adventure.

Finally after three months of labor, I finished. I was so excited and thought about the potential this testimony could have in reaching souls for Jesus. After completing my draft I prayed to God and asked for direction in getting my book out to the world. I prayed many times and asked God for His leading, only to receive silence from the Lord. I had a hard time with this, because I felt the book should go out immediately. I wondered why God was not answering my prayers.

After a month of praying I decided to take matters into my own hands. I figured God must have wanted me to go by faith and reach out to find a publisher. So I sent a copy to Zondervan, a large publishing company that distributes Christian books to practically every bookstore in America. I chose them because they had a solid reputation as a leader in the publishing world.

A few weeks after sending them my manuscript, I received a call from one of their representatives. We had a wonderful chat about my book, and I was greatly encouraged after speaking with him. He loved reading it and said it was uplifting and greatly inspiring. He liked the fact that it covered most of the important subjects Christians are concerned with and loved reading about my supernatural encounters with Jesus. He felt it to be a wonderful resource to use for Bible Study.

He liked it so well, in fact, that he presented it to the board of directors at their next meeting. They discussed the possibilities and decided not to go forward with the project, because my book fell outside their conservative platform.

I was disappointed by their decision, but the fact that they even considered publishing it confirmed that I had achieved my desired intention. I was now confident that I had accurately conveyed in words the wonder and awe of this most unusual testimony.

After receiving the call from the publisher, I went back to the Lord in prayer. I asked God what I should do next, and this time I got my answer. He said I must wait for the appointed time and that I would know in my spirit the time to bring this testimony forth. I heard the voice of the Lord clearly, and with an obedient heart I laid my plans aside and went on with my life.

◆ 14 ◆

It Is Accomplished

Over the next ten years all I did was suffer loss and grief. In the four-season scenario this was going to be an ice age. My marriage dissolved, and my ex moved out of the area. She took my children and moved three hundred miles away. Losing access to my children set the stage for all kinds of grief and sorrow to flood in. My days were filled with deep sadness and depression. I don't want to go into the details, but I will say that I had legal ground in the eyes of God to divorce her. Not wanting to break God's laws I refused to file for divorce. I did not want to be the one to file, so I waited and prayed. She finally filed for divorce, and a few months later our marriage was legally dissolved.

The sorrows of those days were so heavy that I turned back to alcohol as a way to wipe away the pain. I just could not bear the sorrow, and I was willing to do almost anything to shut it off. Those were truly sad days, and I grieve each time I think back on those dark days. I prayed daily for the Lord to take me home and wanted to leave this place of suffering once and for all. But God had other plans for me, and those plans were to prosper me. He was going to give me hope and a future, and He let me know in various ways that He still had big plans for my future.

After years of sadness and suffering, God intervened in my hopeless situation. He delivered me from my fear, my sorrow, and my cruel bondage, and He set my feet on solid ground. As I came out of the darkness, God started filling me with hope, and I suddenly found myself moving forward for the first time in years. It was truly a miracle. I started going to church again and began moving in my gifts that had been shelved for so long.

At this point, God started speaking to me about my book. He had me reread it first. He then led me to make copies to give to the people he wanted to speak to. I gave a copy of my book to everyone God led me to, and everyone got excited. They could clearly see world events and earthly troubles lining up with the visions I had written in my book. All in all, it was truly exciting.

With all these things happening, God began speaking to my heart. The time is at hand for the visions to be fulfilled. The stage is set, and the appointed time is suddenly upon us. The time to publish this book has come. Suddenly it all made sense. If I had published my book years ago, it would now be a fond memory to those who enjoyed reading it. This book is about events soon to take place, so the timing of its release was critical. Soon the visions and the newspapers will be telling the same story, and the people reading my book will know the visions and dreams belong to God and not man.

Knowing the time was at hand, I made a mental inventory of the things I needed to do before I went to the publisher. I needed to have the book edited before publishing it, and I needed to find the money to get the book in print.

Before I sought the funds to pay the publisher, I needed to update my book. Everything had to be accurate and truthful. God wanted me to be completely honest in every way, and this meant telling the truth, the whole truth, and nothing but the truth.

I was married when I wrote this book and could not be honest about our problems without deeply hurting people close to us. I needed to correct that part of the story and explain how God brought this project through to completion. I needed to do this before seeking a publisher, so I sat down at my computer and began the update.

I corrected the story to reflect the truth, and I briefly spoke about the events that took place between the book's completion and now. The book update is finally completed on this day of March 15, 2009. What a miracle it is to be finishing God's book of visions after thirteen years of sitting on a shelf. Now that my book was complete, all I needed was the money to pay the publisher, and then it would be off to the printing press. God had it all worked out in advance and here is how He took care of this hurdle.

Two years ago I took a job working for my old friend Scott in his machine shop in the small town of Graham, Washington. At that time the shop was located on private property in a large garage owned by a man name Dave. Dave leased out his garage to Scott and also did small projects whenever Scott had a need.

Dave and I became instant friends, and God truly had a plan for us meeting. Immediately I began witnessing about the many miracles and visions I have been given. Dave loved hearing about these things, and so it became a daily routine for us to sit and talk about Jesus. We spent untold hours talking about the Lord, and over the next year Dave got on fire for Jesus.

His whole life changed, and he confessed that he thought he had been saved years earlier, but now he knew he was born again. He became so joyful that he said he was almost giddy. I was also enjoying the true joy of the Lord, and we thanked God each day as we lifted Him up in prayer.

This new life started to spill over to his children and even his ex wife. Everyone could see the change in him; this new man was blessing his whole family. He was and is very thankful to me for bringing him back to God, so he started sowing into my life as well. He helped me fix up my home, and he helped me financially when I was in a huge pinch. Dave volunteered to pay for my book to go to press so we contacted the publisher, paid the fees, and left the outcome to God. What a blessing it is to finally say these words, "It is accomplished!"

This is the end of my testimony. I truly hope it blesses you to read about the miraculous God we serve. Over the years, the Lord has given me many endtime visions. I wanted to include them in the story as they occurred but this turned out to be too difficult to manage.

To make these prophetic dreams easier to assimilate, I decided to put them in four different chapters according to the nature of their message. This will make them easy to read and will help you concentrate on the message that God is conveying.

As you read the rest of this book it is important to remember that our God is a loving God who wants all people to come to repentance. Through Jesus, He has provided both salvation and protection. He judges sin, however, with the cup of His fury, which is poured out full strength on those who do not obey the truth. God does this because sin leads to eternal death and must be dealt with and eventually done away with.

May God Himself touch your heart as you read the rest of this testimony, and may the Spirit of truth make plain what the Lord is saying in these last days.

◆ 15 ◆

Endtime Messages

～

The First Trumpet Sounds

"And the first sounded his trumpet: and there was hail and fire, mingled with blood, and they were cast upon the earth; and the third part of the earth was burnt up, and the third part of the trees was burnt up, and all green grass was burnt up" (Revelation 8:7).

In 1994 I had a shocking dream from God that led me to believe that everything written in the Bible about the endtimes is about to be fulfilled. If this dream is valid, and I believe with all my heart that it is, then we must get right with God now, while we still have a chance.

This is the dream, as I received it in July of 1994: I was walking down a sidewalk in what looked to be downtown Seattle. The tall buildings seemed to be empty, and I noticed a few dark-skinned men in each office building watching me as I walked by. I looked to the other side of the street to find that the people in those buildings were also staring at me.

Suddenly, they all left their offices and started to follow me. I guessed that there were about twelve men behind me, but I didn't look back because I did not want them to know I noticed them. I started to get a bit scared, and I began to look for a building to go into for safety.

After that, I saw a door open, and I went in to what looked like the main hallway in a mall. I was glad to be in a public place where I felt safe. I looked back to see if the men were still following me, but I didn't see them. It wasn't until I turned back around that I came face-to-face with them. They were right in front of me, and without saying a word, they surrounded me. I was sure they meant to harm me, but before I could ask them what they wanted, something happened that shocked me.

All of a sudden the power of God came flooding down from above. The men fell to the ground with a thud. Some of them were weeping, some were out cold, and others were shaking all over as God's power kept pouring down on them. As I looked in amazement, I realized that something was going on behind me. I could hear a woman crying as if she had just lost a child. She was weeping and wailing, and I spun around to see what might be the matter. As my eyes focused, I saw this woman lying on the ground, curled up in the fetal position as she kept on crying.

Wanting to know why she was in this condition, I asked, "Lady, why are you crying?" Weeping, she responded, "I have never seen anything like that—it's a miracle! It's a miracle!" I said, "It's the power of God that has done this." She then told me, "You do not understand, those men are Muslims." I responded, "The power of God is going to be poured out on all flesh."

Immediately after I said those words, I heard a loud noise coming from my left. The noise sounded like hundreds of children shouting out as if in a huge, raging battle. I looked towards the direction of the noise to see hundreds of little children running in tight circles. They would burst out suddenly in one direction and circle around in a swirling mass of noise and confusion. I was shocked at this sight; I had never seen anything like it.

As I watched these children, I noticed that they were no more than 3 or 4 years old, and I guessed their number to be at least three hundred. As I watched, something would cause these little children to break out running from the center of the pack. With noisy shrieks they would bolt in one direction and then swirl around in a circular motion. The motion would start from the center of the pack and then work its way out to the perimeter. It looked to me as if they were playing a game like tag. I sat there puzzled at this unusual sight and wondered what it all meant.

As I continued watching, I noticed the children were throwing something they had in their right hands. When I looked down to the ground to see what it was they had thrown, I suddenly had telescopic vision. My eyes zeroed in on what looked like little arrows that were about five inches long and made of a blue-colored plastic. As I examined these arrows I wondered what they might represent, but I got no answer as to their purpose. Later, the Lord told me to read Psalm 18. In verse 14 it says that God shot out his arrows and discomforted the people. I feel this is what the arrows represented, but I'm not going to say definitely because the Lord has not directly revealed this to me.

Suddenly, this mob of children started to move in my direction as they swirled around in what almost looked like some kind of dance. As they came closer, I could feel my heart start to pound out of control. This mob of children slowly moved in front of me, and then, as if by command from above, they all stopped at once and thrust out their right hands with index fingers pointing straight at me. As soon as they pointed at me, a small child appeared out of nowhere and stood about a foot in front of me. I guessed this little child to be about 3 years old due to his height, and to my amazement, he was wearing some kind of mask that covered his whole head.

Before I could react, he pointed his right finger at me and began to speak: "Scott, the first trumpet is about to sound in heaven." He then spoke several words that God would not let me remember. As he continued speaking, the words would go right into my mind and then immediately be taken away. Even though I could not remember the individual words, I do remember that He was telling me about the part I have in warning the people to prepare for the day of the Lord.

The little boy began to quote the book of Revelation to me, word for word, and did so at electronic speed. This shocked me, and I yelled out, "Little children cannot speak the way you do—who are you?" He responded, "Ask God."

As soon as he said these words, a pathway appeared to my left. It led to a door standing open, and I went through this door to find myself in what looked like a football stadium or an outdoor water park. I could see the cement bleachers from a side view that looked much like the ones at a football stadium.

As I looked around, I noticed many people standing around and staring at me as if waiting for me to tell them what to do. I saw lines of people leaning over to see around the crowd as they tried to get a good look at the place I was standing.

Suddenly, a great earthquake struck the area. At the same time I was filled with words from heaven, and they began to pour out of my mouth: "This earthquake is the beginning of sorrows that are to come on this earth." I kept proclaiming, but I cannot remember what God was saying through me.

Suddenly I came bolting out of this dream. As I came to my senses I realized that I was breathing quite heavily, and the power of God was all over me. I was shaking with the very power of God and I could hear two words almost shouted in my head. The two words were, "Ask God." I quickly remembered asking the little boy who he was, and that had been his response. So I said, "God, who is that little boy in this dream?" Immediately God responded, "He represents you."

After hearing this voice, the power subsided, and I lay there in awe. I thought about the little boy and wondered why he had a mask over his head. I started to pray and ask God, and then I heard these words in my head, "Read Jeremiah chapter one." Turning to the first chapter in Jeremiah, I found this: "Then the word of the Lord came unto me, saying, Before I formed thee in the belly I knew thee; and before thou camest forth out of the womb I sanctified thee, and I ordained thee a prophet unto the nations. Then said I, ah, Lord God. Behold, I cannot speak: for I am a child. But the Lord said unto me, Say not, I am a child: for thou shalt go to all that I shall send thee, and whatsoever I command thee thou shalt speak. Be not afraid of their faces: for I am with thee to deliver thee, saith the Lord. Then the Lord put forth his hand, and touched my mouth. And the Lord said unto me, Behold, I have put my words in thy mouth" (Jeremiah 1:4-9).

This scripture depicts my exact feelings about my ability to represent God in the matters of the church. I have always felt like a child inside, and this has made it difficult to carry myself with any measure of confidence. I feel God was saying that He is going to override these feelings, as He did to Jeremiah, by putting His powerful Word inside me and then anointing me with the Holy Spirit to boldly proclaim His Word.

As I was typing this section of my book, I began asking God about the earthquake in this last vision. I felt that it was of the utmost importance to find a biblical reference to an earthquake happening just before the first trumpet sounding. This would give validity to this awesome vision.

On August 18, 1996, while I was on my way to work, the Lord impressed on my heart to listen to the book of

Revelation on cassette tape while I went about my daily routine. I was working alone in a machine shop at the time, and I listened to the Bible on cassette every day. As I began to listen to God's Word, I suddenly knew that God was going to show me something that I needed to see. It took three times through the book of Revelation before I found what I was looking for. Suddenly, my ears caught the information that confirmed what I already knew: "And the angel took the censer, and filled it from the fire of the altar, and cast it on the earth: and there were voices, and thunders and lightnings, and an earthquake. And the seven angels who had the seven trumpets prepared themselves that they might sound with their trumpets. And the first angel sounded his trumpet: and there was hail and fire, mingled with blood, and they were cast upon the earth; and the third part of the earth was burnt up, and the third part of the trees was burnt up, and all green grass was burnt up" (Revelation 8:5-7).

The Whole Earth Shakes

"And they shall go into the holes of the rocks, and into the caves of the earth, for fear of the Lord, and for the glory of his majesty, when he ariseth to shake terribly the earth" (Isaiah 2:19).

One night in January 1994, I went to a church in Seattle to hear a man from Africa preach on endtime subjects. Through his sermon I received interpretations of two visions that God had given me earlier in the year. Excited and full of awe at knowing God's plans in advance, I went home with a feeling of anticipation and fear. That night I prayed with all of my heart before going to bed that God would forgive my foolish ways and use me in His endtime army.

I went to sleep full of the awe of God, only to find myself in a most unusual and upsetting dream. In this dream

I found myself standing on a grassy plain that stretched for what seemed forever. Suddenly, I could see all the mountain ranges of the world at the same time. I was looking through eyes that could somehow see everything up, down, sideways, and backward all at the same time. For some reason I was focused on the mountain ranges of the world. I had never seen such a beautiful sight in all my life, and I was breathless as I examined God's awesome creation with what I now know is the eternal eye of God.

Without warning the mountains started to shake. I was watching the Swiss Alps, the Himalayas, the Cascades, the mountains in Peru, and every other mountain range in the world building force as millions of tons of rock and debris started to move from their timeless positions. I watched as little villages in the Alps became dislodged and began to tumble down the steep slopes so familiar to that area. I was watching from a distance of about half a mile, so I could see the brightly colored buildings with their European architecture collapse before giving way to gravity and tumbling into little splinters of wood.

Then my eyes were directed to one mountain in particular. By this time the earth was shaking so violently that I watched a mountain collapse in sections right down to the ground. One section would fold in to create a sharp ridge. That ridge would then collapse, leaving another shorter ridge that would immediately follow suit as it crashed down. I could see truck-sized rocks flying in every direction, and the noise that was being produced was unimaginable. I remember hearing my voice say, "There is no place for the people to hide, nowhere to hide."

Suddenly, I was overlooking the grassy plain again. This time a man was standing on my right side. As I turned to see him, he started to speak, "Scott, the Unified Countries are about to launch a nuclear strike on American soil. Tell the people to prepare for war." Then the scene changed.

Suddenly, we appeared on a battle scene that I knew to be from World War II. From this point on everything was in black and white just like the old movies. The purpose in viewing this scene without color was unknown. We were standing ten feet away from soldiers who were engaged in hand-to-hand combat, and I watched in horror as one man's stomach was ripped open as a bayonet was thrust into his midsection. I began to convulse at this sight. I then realized that this man had purposely taken me to this place to show me something that I needed to see.

Just then he spoke these words: "Scott, the people of the world are dying and going to hell because they don't know Jesus. Tell them about Jesus." Instantly the scene changed again. I looked to my left, and we were now standing next to a long building that looked something like a hundred-foot long mobile home and having a roof with an unusually steep pitch to it. This building had the look of death to it, and I could see burn marks everywhere, as if it had been on fire. The windows were all broken out; you could smell death everywhere.

The man showing me these things spoke again, saying, "Scott, this is Dachau." Hearing this I felt weak in my stomach, and I turned my eyes away from the building to behold a terrible sight. Just to our right, I saw rows of high poles about ten feet high and about three inches square. Tied to these poles were men who looked like living skeletons. They were completely undressed except for a dirty loincloth. Seeing these men made my heart break.

I watched as a German officer pulled out his pistol. He quickly walked up to the prisoners and began shooting each one of them point blank in the side of the head. He moved fast, and in no time flat the job was finished. I started to vomit at this horrible sight. I was shaking so badly I could not control my hands.

Having watched this most upsetting event, my escort spoke again, "Scott, the people are dying and going to hell because they do not know Jesus. Tell them about Jesus." After that he led me down a steep cobblestone path. Down we went, and I wondered where he was taking me. The path wound around a steep rock cliff as we descended deeper and deeper down the hill. We finally came to a stop right outside a huge door that was also cut out of stone.

The door opened, and we went in. Inside this door was a room that seemed to stretch forever. It looked like a storage building that had a feeling of eternity to it. I then saw what was being stored in this great hall. Neatly stacked were millions of coffins made of what looked like unfinished pinewood. These coffins were just big enough to hold the person inside, and each one was marked with either an X or a Y. I knew these marks represented male and female, but I was not sure which was which. I wondered why someone would go to all the trouble to mark the coffins, and I wondered where these people came from.

Then the man I was with spoke again. "Scott, the people are dying and going to hell because they do not know Jesus. Tell them about Jesus." Instantly, we were out of there and I was standing by a place that I knew was the entrance to hell itself. I saw what looked like a lake made out of some kind of dirty fog. It was dark gray on the surface, and as you looked down it gradually turned black as black can get. It was unpleasant to look at, and I saw what looked like a train trestle leading down into the fog. I knew what I was seeing, and I wanted out of that place as soon as possible.

Then the scene changed one more time. Again we were standing on the same battlefield while the hand-to-hand combat continued. This time I saw another man die at the hands of his enemy. As he fell to the ground, I yelled out, "That man is going to hell because he doesn't know Jesus!"

Suddenly I came out of this dream with my heart pounding and my whole body shaking with fear. This was no pleasant experience. What I saw was beyond my ability to deal with. I knew that God was commanding me to tell the people about Jesus and also about hell. I lay there for some time in a mild state of spiritual shock. Why did I see World War II, and how did this relate to our world today? I had a ton of questions whirling around in my head. This time I knew God was going to be the only one to give me the answers, and that meant I was going to have to start praying like never before.

As I began to pray about these things, God slowly began to give me some answers directly from the Bible. Looking into God's Word, I found many scriptures that describe a time when the whole world will shake, just as I had seen in this vision. Here is one scripture that depicts what I saw: "For the mountains shall depart, and the hills be removed; but my kindness shall not depart from thee, neither shall the covenant of my peace be removed, saith the Lord that hath mercy on thee" (Isaiah 54:10).

The subject of war on America is a tough one to deal with. The Bible clearly states that a nation that turns its back on God will be judged. In God's Word it is clear that He uses nations to judge other nations. Our nation has become God's enemy by promoting all kinds of perversion. We promote homosexual lifestyles as if they were perfectly normal, even though the Bible teaches that this type of sin is an abomination to God. Murder is now an epidemic in some cities, and we let the people that do these things out of prison knowing full well that they will repeat their horrible crimes. At the same time we turn our backs on the victims of violent crimes as though they had no right to safety from such evil criminals. As a nation we also kill millions of babies through abortion each year and then go to church on Sunday to give us a false sense of holiness. This should not be.

How can we escape judgment, when God clearly said in the Bible that a nation that does such things would suffer the penalties prescribed in the Word of God? I have read of men over a century ago having prophecies of America being destroyed by fire (which could be nuclear missiles).

One such prophecy is from a man by the name of Noah Troyer. He was an Amish farmer born in Ohio in 1831. He later moved to Iowa and labored as a farmer and minister for many years. During a serious illness he remained unconscious for a long period of time, during which he repeated a word of warning over and over again. His wife called friends and family to witness what he was saying. She reported that he gave this message nineteen times:

"Just as with Noah before the flood, He is warning me, Noah Troyer, that He is giving America one hundred twenty years to repent before it will be destroyed and it will be too late to repent. People will be partaking of the same sins of fornication, adultery, and homosexuality as they were in the days of Noah when God's wrath was full and He destroyed the earth with a flood. God commanded that they repent and stop their sinning, and instructed Noah to build the ark. He is now giving us one hundred and twenty years to get ready before His wrath will fall on unbelievers and He will rapture the true believers. Then, He will destroy the earth with fire."

This was spoken in the year 1878. Add 120 years, and it comes to 1998.

I too have seen America's judgments in various dreams and visions, and I say amen. America, repent, or be judged by the God who created the heavens and the earth and all that is within them. Even though 1998 has come and gone, the message is still valid. God's Word is going to speak and not lie, and I thank the Lord for His patience. His patience means our salvation, and He is not willing that anyone perish. He truly is a merciful and loving God.

Another area of discussion is my visit to the battlefields of World War II. I continued asking God why He took me there. Slowly I received my answer as I heard prophets and preachers teach on the spirit of the Antichrist and hatred for the Jews. Satan has a plan to wipe out God's children and rule the world through the proposed one world order.

In prayer one day the Lord gave me the understanding that the Antichrist spirit was behind the extermination of the Jews in World War II. That same spirit, God showed me, is alive and active to this day and is going to raise its ugly head one more time. This time it will be all-out war against the saints of God.

God's Spirit Poured Out on the Nations

"And it shall come to pass afterward, that I will pour out my spirit upon all flesh; and your sons and your daughters shall prophesy, your old men shall dream dreams, your young men shall see visions" (Joel 2:28).

In the last hour before the Lord returns, God is going to powerfully visit the earth with His Holy Spirit. The Bible puts it this way: "Be glad then, ye children of Zion, and rejoice in the Lord your God: for he hath given you the former rain moderately, and he will cause to come down for you the rain, the former rain, and the latter rain in the first month" (Joel 2:23).

The former rain represents the outpouring of the Spirit to establish the church. Just before Jesus comes back, the Spirit will be poured out full strength to bring in the great harvest of souls for God. This is what is meant by "the rain, the former rain and the latter rain." In comparison to the first wave of the Spirit, the last and final move of God will be like a tidal wave.

In March of 1993, God showed me this wave of the Spirit in a spectacular dream. I was running from a man who had a shotgun and was going to use it on me. I ran into some thick bushes to hide only to find myself face-to-face with him. He then pointed this gun at me and fired point blank. I was suddenly outside of my body looking down on my corpse that was now missing a head. (I have come to know that dying in these dreams represents change, and in this case it was going to be violent and sudden.)

After a brief examination of my dead body, I began to head skyward. I was ascending at a 45-degree angle, and as I went up, I began to feel the spirit of someone coming from my right. I knew it was a woman and she was ascending up at the same angle, except I was going from left to right, and this woman was moving from right to left, forming a perfect geometric triangle.

We met up in the air and joined together, becoming one in spirit, and suddenly the scene changed. Before our eyes a mountain-sized rock appeared. This mountainous rock was so large, in fact, that it seemed to reach up to heaven itself. I instantly knew that this rock represented Jesus. "And the stone that smote the image became a great mountain, and filled the whole earth" (Daniel 2:35).

Immediately after seeing this great mountain, a huge wave came from the ocean and headed directly at the rock. It hit the side of the rock with the force of a freight train. Then something happened that didn't make sense. Instead of the water splashing against the rock as it normally would, it hit the side of the rock and began climbing the side of this rock mountain as the force of the wave pushed the water higher and higher. I gasped at this sight and wondered how this could be possible.

I watched the water climb to an incredible height, and then it started to come back down with the force of millions of gallons of water as gravity pulled the wave back to earth.

The force that was building as the water rushed back to earth was awe inspiring, and I could see that all the force of this water was being penned up at the base of the rock as if held back by some unseen force.

Then as if a dam had burst, the force built up by the descending water let loose a tidal wave that was unstoppable. This powerful wave was released from the base of the rock, and as the wave went out to the west, our view suddenly changed.

We were high above the state of Washington looking down on the West Coast as if viewing this sight from space. As we looked, we could see that the wave was released from the Washington coastline. This great wave was heading westward, which is directly opposite to the incoming waves on our coast. I could see that the area in which it was released covered the ocean beaches from northern Oregon to central Washington.

Suddenly we were moved to a position that let us watch this powerful wave from the side view. This magnificent wave had the most beautiful crest to it, and it was covering everything in its way. Nothing could escape its path. Even the level of the ocean was being raised by this wave. In front of the wave the sea was at its normal level, and behind the wave the waters had been raised substantially. At that point we were moved up in front of the wave, and we seemed to be propelled forward by its power. It was awe-inspiring; we could see everything being engulfed by this wave. Nothing was too high or too vast to withstand it. The wave swallowed up everything.

Then we were shown all the mountaintops of the world. We could see virtually every mountaintop from the highest mountain ranges in the world to the lowest ranges that are not so well-known. Our eyes then beheld every valley in the entire world. The beauty was overwhelming and I was not sure why I had been shown these sights.

The vision ended with a scene in heaven. We were in a place so beautiful that it was clearly not of this earth. We were hovering in mid air next to a beautiful waterfall. The water looked so pure that it reminded me of the crystal-pond vision. Behind the downpour of water was God's hidden treasure stored up for His saints. My heart cried out to see what was hidden beyond our sight, and my desire to see it was acting like a magnet pulling on my heart. I longed to see what was hidden, but I heard God's voice telling me that I had to wait yet a little while to see my reward. I came out of this dream to find myself back in bed, warmed with the memory of this heavenly vision.

As soon as I awoke, I knew the meaning of this vision. The rock represented Jesus, and the wave was the final move of the Holy Spirit. I believe God was showing me that the last great revival was to begin in the Pacific Northwest and circle the globe from that starting point. I am not sure what will start this wave moving, but I had the feeling that something of biblical proportion was going to set it in motion.

Before the Lord came the first time, he sent John the Baptist to make the crooked road straight for the Lord. He sent him to warn the people that the Lord was coming and to help them prepare their hearts to meet Jesus. The Bible states that Jesus is going to come again, and before His return He would send messengers to make the crooked path straight one more time. Here is the passage that God used to describe this event: "The voice of him that crieth in the wilderness, Prepare ye the way of the Lord, make straight in the desert a highway for our God. Every valley shall be exalted, and every mountain and hill shall be made low: and the crooked shall be made straight, and the rough places plain: And the glory of the Lord shall be revealed, and all flesh shall see it together: for the mouth of the Lord hath spoken it" (Isaiah 40:3-5).

At the time of this vision I had not read this next scripture. When I stumbled across it, I was filled with great joy: "And I will give thee the treasures of darkness, and hidden riches of secret places, that thou mayest know that I, the Lord, which call thee by thy name, am the God of Israel" (Isaiah 45:3).

God Calls His Church Out of the Cities to Escape Destruction

"And the woman fled into the wilderness, where she hath a place prepared of God, that they should feed her there a thousand two hundred and threescore days" (Revelation 12:6).

In September of 1993, God showed me that He would call His church to flee to the east side of the Cascade Mountains, before the destruction of the coastal cities in the Puget Sound region. This is the dream as I received it: I was sleeping soundly when I found myself in the middle of what I knew to be a prophetic dream from the Lord. In this dream the final anointing of power had already been poured out. Filled with the Spirit, I was out boldly preaching the words of God and healing every sick person I could get my hands on. All of a sudden I looked to the north to see that interstate 90 was full of vehicles that stretched for miles on end. I saw every kind of vehicle known to man. These vehicles were bumper to bumper, and the cars, vans and trailers were filled with God's children. I-90 had truly become a highway of holiness as God's children headed east of the mountains. They were fleeing the coastal cities by God's leading to escape the coming destruction. I knew it was time to get out, but this left my heart breaking for the people that remained. Seconds later I woke from this dream with a feeling of sadness that covered my heart. I wondered who would be in this exodus, and I prayed that all my family and friends would be with God's children in the place of safety.

♦ 15 ♦

War on America

"Behold, the eyes of the Lord God are upon the sinful kingdom, and I will destroy it from off the face of the earth; saving that I will not utterly destroy the house of Jacob, saith the Lord" (Amos 9:8).

"For the eyes of the Lord are over the righteous, and his ears are open unto their prayers: but the face of the Lord is against them that do evil" (1 Peter 3:12).

The following visions depict tragic events that are soon to come on this nation. America is going to burn. I am not writing this to scare you, but how can you read these things and not be scared? I am simply trying to warn you of judgments that are already determined against a nation that has turned its back on the one true and living God.

In Deuteronomy 28, the Lord spells out the blessings for obedience and the curses for not following His given laws and precepts. Read it if you want an eye-opener. After you read through, ask yourself if America deserves a blessing or a curse.

As you are reading through this chapter, keep in mind the Lord has promised that everyone who comes to Him with a sincere heart and keeps His commandments will be saved. God will keep His shield of protection around those who love Him and bring them into His kingdom with singing and everlasting joy. In like fashion God will preserve those who come to Him with all their hearts.

From 1991 to 1995 I had the following dreams that confirm what the man had said to me in the vision of World War II. He warned me about the Unified Countries launching a nuclear strike on American soil. The following dreams confirm what was said and should cause all people, "Great and small," to fear God and seek Him while He can still be found.

Russian Submarines off Our Coast

One night I fell asleep to find myself floating high above the country, looking down on America as if it was a map on top of a flat table. I then noticed three black submarines off the Pacific Coast of Washington. I was surprised to see how close they came in. It almost looked as if they had parked on the beach. They were Russian submarines, and I thought they must have found a way to get through our detection devices to get so close to our shores.

Then the scene changed. I suddenly found myself standing on dry ground. I then realized I was standing at the halfway point between Seattle and the coast. With binocular-like vision, I could see both places at the same time. I could see Seattle and the beach as if they were ten feet in front of me.

Without warning, three missiles shot up from the Russian submarines. I watched as these black missiles went straight up into the sky and began to make their arcing turn and deadly descent to hit their intended target.

The first missile seemed to speed up as it made a sharp turn to land directly on the beach. I watched as this powerful bomb exploded, leveling everything for miles. My eyes then turned to the sky to monitor the other missiles. The second missile sped up and turned sharply towards the earth. It exploded midway between the ocean and Seattle.

The third bomb was en route to its destination. At this point I realized that the timing between the explosions was significant. In my mind I reasoned that all three bombs should land at the same time. I somehow understood that the time lag between the explosions meant something. As soon as I realized this, I heard God speak in a way I had never thought possible. Suddenly the whole sky became like a huge speaker and I heard God's voice come forth. He said, "When the third bomb lands, the people must die." After hearing these words I immediately woke from the dream.

Black Jets Attack McChord Air Force Base

In 1991 I had the following dream of an enemy attacking military bases in Washington State. In this dream I was running down the street past my parents' house. I was filled with fear as I kept running and hearing bombs going off all around. A siren was blowing, and I looked up just in time to see a foreign jet pass by at treetop level. This jet was painted black from tip to tail. Its shape and the fact that it was all black confirmed to me that it was not one of ours.

I ducked behind some bushes thinking there might be foreign troops in the area. Seconds later I heard bombs explode near McChord Air Force Base some two miles from my parent's home. Hearing these explosions I knew the enemy had hit his mark. Shocked, I came bolting out of this nightmare and lay there for some time wondering who had attacked us.

Nuclear Bombs Destroy Our Cities

In January of 1995 I had a dream that American cities were being destroyed by nuclear bombs. I found myself in a dream where I witnessed a nuclear attack on what I knew to be a city in the United States. Even though I did not know what city it was, I felt that it was one of our coastal cities. I watched as one bomb exploded to the south of this city, causing unbelievable damage. The bomb had landed quite a bit south of the city, so most of the buildings were still intact after the explosion. The sad thing is that the people had run into the skyscrapers thinking they would be safe due to the size of these buildings. I saw another bomb land and rip right through these giant buildings as if they were made of paper.

Then the scene changed. Some time had passed in the sequence of events, because I could see some buildings still standing, and the city was burning out of control. I began to walk through the city, encased in what looked like a bubble that protected me from the flames. I could see this bubble clearly. It looked like a ten-foot-high, crystal-clear balloon.

As I walked through the city, my heart grew faint from the destruction, and I wondered how anyone could justify doing something so evil. I kept walking north until I reached a building that was still half standing. I went inside to find some people still alive. They were all down on the ground barely breathing. Moved by this, I cried out loud, "Who has done this to us?" After asking this question I waited in silence but got no clear answer.

Washington State under Nuclear Attack

In March of 1995 I had an alarming dream that depicted Russia sending nuclear bombs to destroy certain targets in western Washington State. In this dream I was running some errands in the city of Auburn, about fifteen miles south of

Seattle. All of a sudden the air raid sirens sounded, followed by nuclear missiles coming down from the skies headed for their intended targets.

After the bombs landed I witnessed total panic as people were trying to get to their cars and escape the area. I had survived the blast, and everything inside me wanted to get back home and see if my parents were OK. I also had hopes that I would get back to Tacoma to find the city untouched.

I made my way back home by hitching a ride in a military truck. When I arrived I found that the military had blocked off the main roads. I got to my parents' home to find they were all right, but I then had to leave because the military began rounding up people to evacuate the city.

I was waiting in a long line of people who were to be evacuated when I noticed a group of military personnel being briefed by the side of the road. I went over in time to hear what the officer was saying. He was telling his men that the United States had just launched a total and complete counterstrike that was going to totally blow Russia off the face of the planet. He said Russia had also launched most of its missiles in response to ours, but the top military leaders felt confident that we could survive this all-out attack, at least in part.

Having said that he showed his men a map highlighting the three main regions the Russians had destroyed in their first round of attack. I watched as he pointed to the three areas circled in red. He used a pointer to locate the area he was discussing, and he described the amount of damage to each area: the city of Everett and its suburbs, the Auburn valley where the Boeing plant is located, and the whole city of Bremerton, including the naval shipyards. The commanding officer told his men these areas had been totally destroyed.

The officer wished his men Godspeed. Then he outlined the plan to evacuate the city in a futile attempt to escape the next wave of nuclear bombs that were already on their way. I decided to sit still and wait for the inevitable. I was going to meet my Maker in just a few short minutes. I sat motionless in a state of prayer as I wondered how it was going to feel to be vaporized by a hundred-megaton bomb.

Alaska, the Doorway to America

In September of 1995 I had a dream revealing that military troops are going to come through Alaska to attack the mainland. I watched three nuclear bombs land on American soil. I did not see where they landed, and I was not told who sent them our way. I was inside this huge hotel, and I noticed that the people seemed oblivious to the attack. They went on eating, drinking, and having fun.

I then realized that I was not in my home state of Washington. I walked outside to see barren, tundra-like hills that had little vegetation. I realized I was in Alaska. I then noticed a large channel of water with two military ships anchored out in the deepest part and I turned around to see that I was standing on a helicopter launching pad next to a small military outpost.

Under the cover of camouflage, four helicopters were sitting on a hangar pad. Three of them had clearly been stripped for parts, and it looked a bit like a junkyard instead of a functioning military outpost. These three helicopters had been stripped of their engines, doors, and rotor blades.

The fourth helicopter had lots of used parts on it. The pilot's door was a different color from the rest of the aircraft, and the cowlings around the nose were obviously from some other craft. It was a pathetic sight. I realized that our military resources had been cut so badly they had to resort to these extreme cost-cutting measures.

Out of the corner of my eye I noticed something floating down slowly from the sky. I turned to see that it was a parachute, and I watched it land about two hundred yards in front of me. That is when I figured out what was actually happening. Out from under the parachute came a man with a machine gun. I couldn't tell which country he was from, but I knew this was no military exercise.

After that, hundreds of parachutes came down and littered the hillsides with troops. They grouped in little bands, then spread out and surrounded the building that housed the helicopters. At this point I wanted to shout. We were being attacked, and there were no American troops in sight to defend our base. I was furious and looked out to the ships to see what kind of defense they would mount. I kept watching but saw nothing at all. The ships seemed to be deserted. What was going on? Where were our troops?

By this time I could see that the enemy had figured out the same thing. Suddenly they stood straight up and began to walk in the direction of their intended target. I watched as they approached from below, and then I suddenly awoke from this upsetting dream.

♦ 16 ♦

Natural Disasters and the Endtimes

≈

"And I will plead against him with pestilence and with blood; and I will rain upon him, and upon his bands, and upon the many people that are with him, an overflowing rain, and great hailstones, fire, and brimstone" (Ezekiel 38:22).

"When thou didst terrible things which we looked not for, thou camest down, the mountains flowed down at thy presence" (Isaiah 64:3).

The Bible says that in the last days God will plead against the sins of mankind to force men to repent from their evil ways and turn to Him for healing and salvation. Because men's hearts have become hardened by sin, God will have to use all kinds of pressure to do this. Ezekiel 38:22 refers to God using pestilence and blood to draw men to repentance. We currently see various countries plagued with pestilence and famine. The AIDS virus has now gripped the nations and is an issue of blood that has many people crying out for relief and healing.

Another form of pleading that God will use is natural disasters. In the past few years we have seen flood after flood devour whole regions. Fires burn out of control and hurricanes are pounding our coastlines in ever-increasing measure. God is using all these things to get a hard-hearted people to cry out to Him. The following dreams are vivid pictures of upcoming disasters.

The West Coast Breaks Off and Slips into the Sea

In October of 1994 I had a dream that depicted a kind of disaster that I had never before considered or thought about. I was standing on the edge of what looked like a five-hundred-foot cliff, steeply sloping down to the edge of the Pacific. The dirt sloping down to the water looked fresh. It was light brown, and you could tell that this dirt had not been exposed to the wind and rain normally associated with cliffs by the sea. I also noticed that no vegetation whatsoever could be found on this cliff, which was abnormal by any standard. This was unusual, and I gasped at the sight of it.

Then I noticed something by my feet that gave me insight into what had happened. The grass was growing right up to the edge of the cliff. It looked as if it had been torn off at the cliff's edge. I realized what had happened—I was standing on the edge of a whole new coastline. The land that had once bordered the ocean had broken off and slipped into the sea.

I frantically began to look around to get a bearing on where I was standing. I knew this was the West Coast, but I saw no discernible landmarks that would give me a clue as to where I was standing.

After looking all around, my eyes then focused on a terrible sight. Coming in from the west, I saw a mountain of water rushing at the coastline with an unstoppable momentum. At this point I was taken up into what looked like a high tower. It looked like the towers the Coast Guard uses to watch for boats in trouble and monitor the activities around harbors.

In this tower I could see huge tidal waves heading directly for the coast. I held on as they began to pound the land with unbelievable force. One after another they came in. I tried to count them but was unable to because the tower was covered by the first wave and I couldn't do anything from that point on except hold on for dear life. I remember seeing at least seven waves, and it seemed that the third wave was much larger than the others. It towered above the rest of the waves; its sight was utterly terrifying. After seeing this wave, I closed my eyes and prayed. I then came out of this dream to find myself physically shaking.

Mount St. Helens Erupts Again

On May 11, 1994 (a week before the anniversary of the May 18, 1980 eruption of Mount St. Helens) I had a spectacular dream. Unaware of the date, I was surprised to have a dream about this volcano erupting one more time. I was standing five miles away from a mountain whose top was concealed by an unusual cloud. The cloud was oval in shape and totally covered the mountaintop, so I could not tell which mountain I was looking at. I realized this cloud was different from clouds in the sky; it looked more like a thick fog mixed with yellow and black smoke.

Suddenly from inside this cloud came continuous flashes of lightning that lit up the whole cloud from the inside out. These lightning bolts were different than any I had seen, because instead of shooting down from the sky, these bolts shot sideways in horizontal streaks and seemed to stop at the outer edge of the cloud. I watched in amazement as these bolts of lightning increased in intensity, and it looked as if the cloud itself was almost boiling above the mountain.

Then, without warning, the whole mountain exploded right down to the ground. I watched as a trillion tons of rock and debris went up in the air with a huge fireball directly behind. I had never thought about the possibility of a whole mountain disappearing in an instant, but this one exploded with such force that the only thing left after the blast was a huge crater. The fireball that came out of this explosion went out in every direction. I watched in awe as huge columns of flames boiled up from the ground as it purged its fury into the atmosphere after the explosion. I watched tons of rock and debris fall from the sky. Then an eerie, unsettling silence fell. I sat there dumbfounded. I then heard my voice ask a question: "What mountain was that—which mountain blew?"

I was not able to see the top of the mountain because it was covered with that cloud. This made identification impossible and left me wondering. As soon as I asked this question two things happened simultaneously.

I heard a man's voice say, "Mount St. Helens." At the same time, I watched the scene before me change in two movements. It looked like a slideshow. One slide, another slide, and then the third slide came into focus to reveal Mount Rainier.

The final scene in this dream was a perfect picture of Mount Rainier—the sky, the snow, everything looked as peaceful as ever, and I knew God was showing me that Mount St. Helens was going to blow before Mount Rainier.

Mount Rainier Destined to Blow

Two weeks after having the dream of Mount St. Helens exploding, I had a dream that Mount Rainier erupted. In this dream I was in the Auburn valley standing along the west banks of the Green River. It was a beautiful day, and I saw Mount Rainier standing as peaceful as ever. Suddenly I felt the ground below me start to soften, and I looked down in horror to see the sand on the banks of the river starting to expand like heated-up oatmeal. I ran up the banks of the river to find solid ground, and then I saw what was causing the ground to boil.

As I looked to the east, I saw Mount Rainier spewing huge rocks and debris out of the center of its crater. I was shocked senseless, and I had to clear my eyes and take one more look before I could believe what I was seeing. At this point I felt a very slight earth tremor and noticed something that looked like small sparks mixed with the rocks that were being thrown into the air from the mountain.

This was a totally different kind of eruption from Mount St. Helens, because Mount Rainier had little ash coming out of its crater. I immediately noticed this and wondered why the two mountains erupted in totally different ways. This dream ended as I was making my way to higher ground to escape the destructive mudslides already on their way down the mountainsides.

In May of 1996, my good friend Scott and I attended a U.S. Geological Survey meeting in the town of Orting, Washington. The purpose was to inform the public of the various hazards that Mount Rainier posed to the towns in the valleys around its base.

During this meeting, the history and nature of our native volcanoes was discussed in detail. I learned that eruptions in the Cascade ranges occur at the rate of one or two per century. Mount St. Helens has been the most active volcano in the state, erupting fifteen times in the last four thousand years. According to the speaker at this meeting, Mount St. Helens will most definitely be the next mountain to erupt.

In 1995 it was thought that Mount St. Helens was going to blow again. Scientists monitored hundreds of little earthquakes just under the mountain, and this information pointed to the fact that a huge gas bubble was building under the mountain. They were concerned that this bubble would ignite and explode with the force of many nuclear bombs, which could reduce the mountain to a great cloud of ash.

Each mountain erupts in a different way, according to the type of soil and rock found in the area. Mount Rainier and Mount St. Helens are totally different in both their rock and soil composition. The speaker informed us that a Mount Rainier eruption would look completely different from the eruptions of Mount St. Helens.

When Rainier erupts, little ash is likely to be seen coming from the top of the mountain. Instead of ash it's likely that huge rocks will shoot out of the mountain, and mudslides will flow down the slopes. The rocks are called bombs and are typical in the type of eruptions that are known to occur with the type of soil and rock found in the area surrounding Mount Rainier.

♦ 17 ♦

A Call to Holiness

"And then shall appear the sign of the Son of man in heaven: and then shall all the tribes of the earth mourn, and they shall see the Son of man coming in the clouds of heaven with power and great glory" (Matthew 24:30).

In the spring of 1994 God gave me two dreams that seem to be interconnected. These two dreams sum up and complete the message of this book, and I pray that you will take to heart this entire testimony. I would also urge you to look into the Bible to see if these visions line up with the overall prophetic picture detailed in God's Word. God commands us to test the spirits and wants us to test each word of prophecy against His living Word for validity. After you do this search and combine it with much prayer, I am confident that God will grant you insight into the truths contained in these dreams.

I went to sleep as usual one night to find myself in a fantastic and awe-inspiring dream about the Second Coming of Jesus Christ. I was fishing alongside a river and noticed a black man fishing next to me. I caught a beautiful silver salmon and laid it on the ground to examine it. As I looked at this fish, the man came over to see what I had caught. As we discussed this fish, I decided to give it to him as a friendly gesture.

I told him I wanted him to have it, but he declined my offer. He then told me the fish was a gift from the Lord and that God wanted me to have it. As soon as he said this, the fish turned into a pure white bunny rabbit. It had a purity that could only come from heaven. I was stunned at this unusual sight and wondered what it could represent.

Seconds later, the rain started to come down from above. It started out fairly normal, but as the rain kept coming down, it began to warm as if coming out of a showerhead. As the temperature increased, the size of the raindrops began to increase. This casual rain became a downpour of record proportion. The rain increased in intensity as these huge raindrops were pelting everything. Then, as if God Himself opened the faucet to maximum flow, the raindrops increased in size again. This time the raindrops expanded to the size of a softball. These huge drops were pounding the earth with the intensity of a thousand storms—and they were filled with an electrical charge. These huge drops of warm water were pounding me, and as they covered me with their warmth, I was also being energized by an electrical current that felt like golden oil.

I tilted my head back, threw my arms open, and just soaked in this golden electricity. This heavenly outpouring was covering the whole earth, and nothing could escape being covered by these unusual drops of liquid electricity.

Then I heard a voice shake the heavens and the earth. I heard a commanding male voice proclaim, "Look up!" I opened my eyes and looked up into the cloud-covered sky. As I looked up, I saw thick, dark clouds and I knew the golden raindrops had come from these strange and unusual clouds.

Then the clouds began to move. I watched as these boiling clouds suddenly drew back like a curtain. Behind them I could see Jesus Christ coming with great glory and power. This dream ended with my eyes on Jesus and my heart ready for glory. I woke from this awesome dream wondering if the world would believe what the Bible taught about the Second Coming of Christ.

I found an Old Testament scripture that speaks about an endtime downpour of the Holy Spirit: "Be glad then, ye children of Zion, and rejoice in the Lord your God: for he hath given you the former rain moderately, and he will cause to come down for you the rain, the former rain, and latter rain in the first month" (Joel 2:23). This outpouring will affect the entire world and is one of the events that will precede the coming of the Lord.

Two weeks after this I was given another dream from above. This last dream is one that stirs my heart to press more and more into the things of God while there is still time. I went to sleep as usual, only to find myself in a most spectacular vision. I call it a vision because I was fully conscious as if wide awake, with all my faculties in full operation.

I was floating high up in the upper atmosphere, in a beautiful, azure-blue sky. I was fully awake. I noticed I was in the center of a huge tunnel of clouds. It was at least ten miles wide and stretched ahead of me for what seemed an eternity.

The clouds were so beautiful and reminded me of a very old painting done by a master painter. The edges of the clouds were pronounced and majestic, and looked as if they were as old as time.

After a few seconds, a brilliant light broke out from the center of the tunnel. Far ahead of me and in the center of the tunnel came a light so bright that the sun paled by comparison. I tried to look at this intense light, but its brilliance was too great. This light was in the shape of a cross, but I could barely make out the shape as I strained my eyes to see.

Then, as if touched by God, my eyes suddenly adjusted to the light, and I was able to look directly into it. As I focused on the cross, I was shocked to find the source of this great light was Jesus. He was standing with his arms outstretched as if He was still on the cross, and He was glowing with the radiance of a thousand suns. He looked like metal glowing in a furnace that was heated up a thousand times over.

Immediately after seeing Jesus, my eyes turned back to the clouds. As I reexamined these timeless clouds, I began to see with sight beyond the earthly realm. As I looked, I saw what these clouds really were. They were formed by billions and billions of people all dressed in white robes. They were assembled before the Lamb of God, Jesus, and they were all facing Him as if in a great assembly. All eyes were on Jesus. I am convinced that if I could have seen the clouds from a different angle, I would have seen billions of palm branches in the hands of the saints of God.

Waking from this awesome vision, I was moved deep within my heart. These last two dreams were living pictures from the Bible. The messages contained in these two dreams go hand-in- hand. First of all, Jesus is on His way back to receive all the people who are waiting patiently for His Second Coming. And the second vision is a picture of where all of those saints are going when He finally does arrive—heaven.

In the book of Revelation I found a scripture that describes this second vision exactly. "After this I beheld, and, lo, a great multitude, which no man could number, of all nations, and kindreds, and people, and tongues, stood before the throne, and before the Lamb, clothed with white robes, and palms in their hands" (Revelation 7:9).

The Bible is trustworthy and true. Every prophecy written in God's Word is being fulfilled without exclusion. In the Old Testament we see God's promises of a Messiah sent to die for the sins of the world. With the virgin birth of Jesus, hundreds of prophetic words were fulfilled. Every detail happened exactly as the Bible said it would.

Then Jesus went to the cross, just as the Bible said He would. He died on the cross to pay the penalty for our sins, and three days later He rose from the dead. After that He showed Himself to more than five hundred people as a witness and testimony to the truths written in God's Word. You can read about these events in Roman history books. Their archives contain writings about Jesus as part of a historical record that was not written from a religious perspective.

Having shown Himself to the people, Jesus ascended to the right hand of the Father in great glory. Before He left this earthly realm, He gave us this one promise to hold on to. He promised: "In my Father's house are many mansions: if it were not so, I would have told you. I go to prepare a place for you. And if I go and prepare a place for you, I will come again, and receive you unto myself; that where I am, there ye may be also" (John 14:2-3).

Jesus is coming back. The Bible is God's living Word and declares that He has risen. Because He lives, He is going to come again to receive all who put their trust in Him. If Jesus had not risen, our faith would be in vain and useless. Jesus secured the victory over death, hell, and the grave when He rose from the dead. The tomb that contained His body is empty to this very day.

The Bible teaches the only way to Heaven is through Jesus and His shed blood on the cross. Jesus said, "I am the way, and the truth, and the life: No one cometh unto the Father, but by Me" (John 14:6). It also declares that our good works are like filthy rags and none of us is worthy of heaven: "As it is written, There is none righteous, no, not one" (Romans 3:10).

So, if you are going to rely on your good works to get you into heaven, you are going to be very disappointed. You will only stand at the Great White Throne of Judgment to be shown just how sinful you really were, as God pronounces your eternal sentence of punishment.

Even our best behavior is like filth compared to the righteousness of God. Nothing we think or do or say is worthy to dwell in heaven. That is why Jesus had to come in the first place. When we receive Jesus, we take on His righteousness and are accepted by God. Jesus Christ has already paid for the sin penalty, which is death. He died in our place and then was raised to eternal life.

By receiving Jesus, we also died and were resurrected two thousand years ago on the same cross. The word *gospel* means "good news." This is good news because getting to heaven no longer depends on our behavior and what we think and do. It now relies completely on Jesus and what He did for us. God accepted His sacrifice and then accepts all that come to Him though His Son, Jesus. And that is what I call Good News indeed.

Now that you have read this book and have been told the truth, you have a choice to make. You can believe what the Bible teaches about God's Son, Jesus, or you can reject it. You can mock and scoff or you can believe and receive.

The Bible teaches that unless we believe the gospel and repent, we cannot be saved. The word *repent,* means to "change one's mind." God wants us to read His book, the Bible, and live the way He commands in His Word. The Bible says, "Know ye not, that to whom ye yield yourselves servants to obey, his servants ye are to whom ye obey; whether of sin unto death, or of obedience unto righteousness" (Romans 6:16).

The Bible teaches that without holiness a man cannot see God. Holiness means to be dedicated, consecrated, and separated. "Come out of the world all you who love the Lord and be ye separated. Come out of her and share not in her judgment. Wash your robes all you sinners and be washed in the blood of the Lamb."

By following God's ways we will be blessed in what we do, and we will have peace, knowing that we are pleasing God by obeying His commandments. We will also enjoy the safety that we have in living holy lives.

You have read what happened to me because of my sinful ways. I would have been spared years and years of grief if I had only known what the Bible taught about living a holy life. I believe with everything in me that I would have listened and changed my ways. I thank God that He helped me to see the truth before it was too late. I am still suffering the consequences of my sins, but I am now living life the way the Bible commands. I am blessed beyond measure, knowing that Jesus is my Lord and Savior and heaven will be my eternal home.

If you have just read this book and have not yet trusted Jesus as Lord and Savior, listen closely. The time to ask Jesus into your heart is at hand. I don't care what you have done in the past. The Bible says that we have all sinned and fallen short of the glory of God. Not one human being is worthy of heaven—not one. That is why Jesus had to come and die for us.

The Bible teaches, "God so loved the world, that he gave his only begotten Son, that whosoever believeth in him should not perish, but have everlasting life" (John 3:16). Jesus came down from heaven. He is God in the flesh, born of a virgin. He came to this earth for one purpose, and that was to die for our sins so we will not have to go to hell. He did it because He loves us. Anyone who accepts Jesus as Lord and Savior will enter into an eternal home called heaven, while everyone who rejects Jesus and His sacrifice will be sent to hell.

Hell is a place of eternal separation from God's love and presence. In hell there is no light, no rest, no comfort, and absolutely no hope of anything good for all eternity. God created hell as a prison for Satan and his demons, not for man. When a person follows Satan and refuses the free gift of salvation found only in Jesus Christ, God has no other choice but to send him to that terrible place. To put it another way, if you go to hell you go willingly. You sent yourself by not believing the truth. You choose your own destiny, and this is as fair as it gets.

The Bible also teaches that everyone in hell will eventually be cast into the lake of fire. This is an eternal place burning with fire and brimstone, and the Bible teaches that the occupants of this lake will be in torment forever and ever. It breaks God's heart to have to do this, but He has already done all He can possibly do to save us by sending His Son, Jesus, to die in our place. If you reject Jesus and His sacrifice on the cross, you are rejecting God's plan of salvation, leaving Him with no other option. The Bible puts it this way: "The Lord is not slack concerning His promise, as some men count slackness, but is longsuffering toward us, not willing that any should perish, but that all should come to repentance" (2 Peter 3:9).

The Word of God clearly states "It is appointed unto men once to die, but after this the judgment" (Hebrews 9:27). Reincarnation, purgatory, and second chances are all lies from the father of lies, Satan. Salvation is only found in God's Son, Jesus, and the blood He shed on Calvary's cross. All who believe in Jesus shall live. If you repent and turn your life over to Jesus, you too will "share in the tree of life that is in the Paradise of God."

Jesus said: "All that which the Father giveth me shall come unto me; and him that cometh to Me I will in no wise cast out" (John 6:37). If this book has stirred your heart, it is because God Himself is pulling on your heartstrings. The time to enter God's kingdom has come. It is time to turn your life over to Jesus. If you have already received Him, begin to pursue your high calling with all your heart. Fast and pray for direction and protection. If you have never received Jesus as Lord and Savior and would like to, then pray this simple prayer:

"O heavenly Father, I am a sinner. I know that I am lost and cannot save myself, but I just read that there is hope for people like me. I just read that Jesus Christ is my hope. I read that if I receive Jesus as Lord and Savior, I will be saved. I read that if I come to Jesus, He will not turn me away. So I come now, Jesus. Forgive me for my sins and come into my heart. Help me to live a godly life the way the Bible teaches, and help me to clean up my life and live holy. Thank You for saving me, thank You for cleansing me, and thank You for dying on the cross so that I might live."

If you just prayed that prayer and meant it, you are now a member of the body of Christ. This is God's greatest miracle, and even now the angels are rejoicing over your victory in Jesus. Now that you are a born-again Christian, you need to start reading your Bible to find out who you are in Christ Jesus. Get to know God's nature and pray continually. Go to a good, solid church that preaches the whole Word of God. All of the things I have written about are for you too, so believe for great things and see what the Lord will do.

With your salvation in hand, I will now end this book. I have finished my purpose in writing this testimony and will be looking forward to meeting you in eternity to rejoice over our victory.

God bless you—both now and forever!

Your brother in Christ,
Scott Madsen

Printed in the United States
151117LV00001B/125/P

9 781607 917243